INSHORE FLIES

INSHORE FLIES

Best Contemporary Patterns
from the Atlantic and Gulf Coasts

JIM SCHOLLMEYER
and **TED LEESON**

Frank Amato
PORTLAND

All inquiries should be addressed to:
Frank Amato Publications, Inc.
P.O. Box 82112 • Portland, Oregon 97282 • 503-653-8108
www.amatobooks.com

Book Design: Amy Tomlinson
Photography: Jim Schollmeyer

Printed in Hong Kong
1 3 5 7 9 10 8 6 4 2

Softbound ISBN: 1-57188-193-X
Spiral Hardbound ISBN: 1-57188-194-8

Softbound UPC: 0-66066-00404-8
Spiral Hardbound UPC: 0-66066-00405-5

TABLE OF CONTENTS

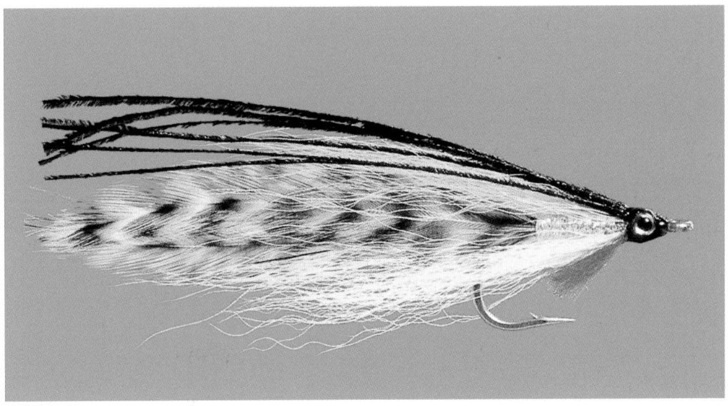

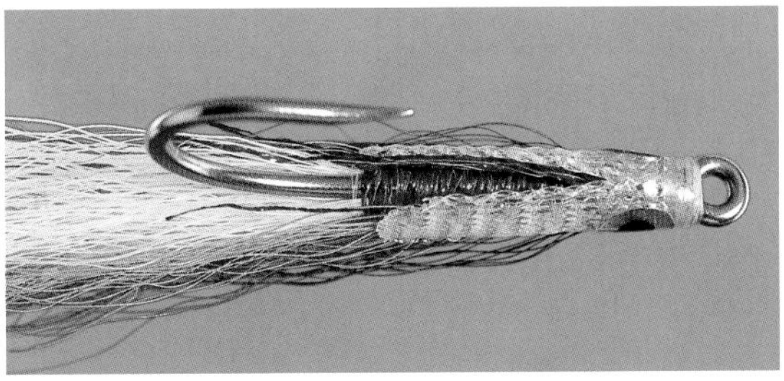

Introduction

The evolution of saltwater fly fishing has been both a recent phenomenon and a rapid one. Just a few decades ago, it was considered the province of a lunatic fringe, an esoteric sport for a handful of experts, a pioneer's game. Today, saltwater angling is not only enormously popular, but the fastest growing segment of fly fishing as anglers travel to parts of the world and pursue a range of species that Izaak Walton never dreamed of. Their continued observations and experimentation have led to an improved understanding of the resource—the life cycles, habits, and migratory patterns of both the game fish and their prey—and this knowledge has, in turn, sparked a tremendous burst of creative energy among fly tyers. As saltwater fly fishing flourishes, saltwater tyers bring an increasing vitality and inventiveness to their craft.

As always in fly tying, the innovation takes place on a local level, as individual tyers design and refine patterns for use on their home waters. *Inshore Flies: Contemporary Patterns from the Atlantic and Gulf Coasts* is one of a series of books devoted to presenting these patterns—designed by knowledgeable anglers in a given area and sold through local fly shops for use in surrounding waters—to a larger audience of tyers. Like its companion volumes, *Trout Flies of the West* and *Trout Flies of the East*, this book has two purposes. First, it is intended as a resource for anglers who live in or will travel to particular coastal regions and wish to equip themselves with proven flies, the "shop patterns" recommended for the area. Second, as fly anglers know well, a pattern than is productive in one part of the country is often just as effective elsewhere. A redfish pattern that is a local favorite in Florida may prove just the ticket in Texas; a striped bass fisherman in Virginia may find effective fly designs from tyers in Maine. A creative idea, a new fly style is often the answer when more conventional patterns fail, and we hope that the flies shown here can provide anglers and tyers with fresh approaches wherever they may live.

To compile this book, we contacted fly shops in the Atlantic and Gulf coast states and asked them to contribute patterns designed and tied for their local waters. The response was enthusiastic and generous, and the flies that appear in these pages represent general attractor patterns, imitations of specific food forms, and just about everything in between; some employ traditional natural materials, while others incorporate the latest in synthetics. In aggregate, they demonstrate the wealth of creative talent and knowledge that is found among saltwater fly tyers.

About This Book

To make this book as useful as possible to tyers, we have shown many of the flies from more than one angle since the simple side-view customarily used in pattern books does not always provide the kind of detail necessary to reproduce a fly at the vise. For each pattern, the main photograph (on a green background) generally pictures the fly in profile; supplementary photos (on a blue background) show selected patterns from the top, underside, and/or front as a way of illustrating more clearly the proportions, placement, or arrangement of material on the hook shank. In some cases, these supplementary photos show alternate colors, color combinations, or materials recommended by the originator or tyer. Similarly, the "Comments" section that accompanies the pattern may contain brief instructions from the tyers themselves about dressing the pattern or some of its less-familiar components. And because tying a fly is really the starting point, rather than the endpoint, of fishing, the "Comments" sections frequently contain information from the tyer or contributing shop about where, how, or under what circumstances the fly can be fished most effectively.

For convenient reference, we've organized the patterns by geographical region to accommodate anglers who are tying for a specific destination. For those interested tying flies for a particular species, we have included a "Pattern/Species Index" at the back of the book that cross-references the fly patterns with the varieties of fish for which they are used. This index was compiled from information provided by the tyers and shop owners, who indicated the one or two primary species for which a pattern was designed, as well as additional species for which it's proven effective. Thus virtually all of the fly patterns appear under more than one species category in the index, but it's worth remembering that establishing such categories is an uncertain and imprecise business since a great number of patterns tend to cross boundaries. One man's tarpon fly may be another man's shark fly, and paging through this book to get an idea of the range of fly styles and designs may be the best way to discover a pattern that meets your needs.

About the Flies

The patterns in this book are all designed primarily for inshore saltwater fishing, though again, such boundaries are not easily fixed. Many of the patterns shown here are also suitable for offshore fishing and, in appropriate sizes and colors, for fishing freshwater species such as largemouth, smallmouth, and peacock bass, pike, and even trout. But the versions pictured here are those that contributing shops and tyers have found most successful for inshore fishing.

Since there is an entry under each pattern for the "originator" of the fly, a word of explanation is in order. Some patterns in this book are variations of more familiar fly styles. In such cases, we have listed the "originator" as the tyer who devised the specific version that is pictured, with the understanding that most tyers will recognize the fly as an adaptation of a well-known design—as a variation of Lefty Kreh's Deceiver, for instance. And in fact many of the submitting shops and tyers strongly emphasized that their patterns were variations rather than wholly original designs. As many of the tyers pointed out to us, the originator of pattern can be difficult to determine, since fly patterns tend to evolve continually. Except for those patterns of unknown origin, however, we have credited an originator for each fly as a way of acknowledging either a tyer's adaptation of an existing design or, as is the case with many of the patterns shown here, a tyer's largely original dressing.

In putting together a series of three books focused on contemporary fly patterns, we have had the opportunity to inspect thousands of flies and read thousands of fly pattern recipes. It's clear from this experience that saltwater tyers face two particular obstacles far more frequently than trout-fly dressers. The first is materials. There are an enormous number of synthetic materials available today, and saltwater tyers draw freely upon the entire range of them. In the recipes that accompany each pattern, some tyers have been emphatic about the use of specific materials, while others have been less insistent on such matters. Readers, of course, are free to substitute or alter materials as they choose, but those seeking to reproduce as closely as possible the pattern as it is pictured may at times run into some less commonly available materials or trade names that are not familiar, particularly when synthetics are involved. In almost every case, such materials are readily available from the contributing shops. The second obstacle is in the complexity of some dressings. While many of the patterns in this book are quite straightforward, some of them are more complicated—less for any specialized techniques that are required than for the large number of materials applied to the hook in a specific sequence. We believe that the photographs, and in many cases written instructions, will enable tyers to reproduce the patterns. Some tyers, though, may desire a sample pattern to use as a model, and like the materials, these are available from the contributing shops. These shops are listed in a directory at the end of the book. A large number of them can also assist in arranging guides, casting instruction, and other destination services, and they are a valuable resource for anglers traveling throughout the eastern and southern United States.

Finally, we would like to extend our deepest thanks to the shops and tyers who generously shared their patterns, tying techniques, information, and enthusiasm for this project. Designing effective fly patterns often requires significant time, trial and error, and persistence, and we are grateful to the tyers who gave us the benefit of their experience.

CHAPTER 1

New England States

Maine – Massachusetts – New Hampshire

Bead Chain Fly

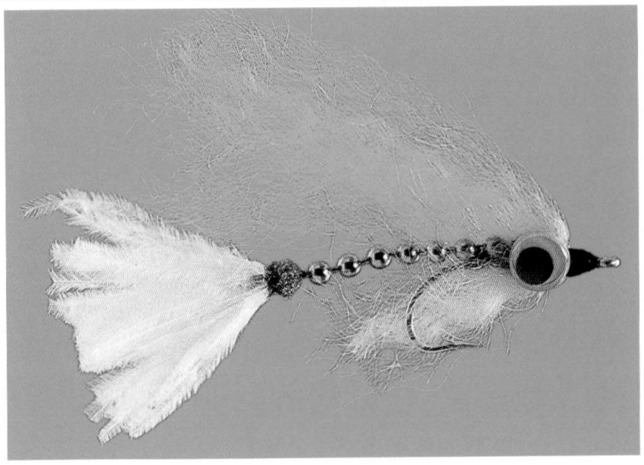

Overall length: 3 1/2″ on #1/0 hook
Pattern type: Attractor, baitfish
Primarily designed for: Striped bass, bluefish
Submitted by: The Bear's Den Fly Fishing Shoppe (Taunton, Massachusetts)
Originated by: Joel Swan
Tied by: Joel Swan

Hook: Mustad 34007, #1-#1/0
Thread: Black monofilament
Tail: White ostrich herl
Body: Silver bead chain
Wing: Seafoam green Kinky Fiber (or suitable substitute)
Belly: White Kinky Fiber (or suitable substitute)
Eyes: Doll eyes

Benoit's Patriot Popper

Overall length: 4″ on #1 hook
Pattern type: Attractor
Primarily designed for: Striped bass
Submitted by: Eldredge Bros. Fly Shop (Cape Neddick, Maine)
Originated by: Brett Benoit
Tied by: Brett Benoit

Hook: Mustad 34011, #1
Thread: White Flymaster Plus
Tail: Red Fly Fur and frayed end of body tubing
Underbody: Wapsi #2 popper body, 1/4″ trimmed from rear before gluing
Overbody: Large pearl Mylar tubing, fray excess at rear for tail; top of body colored with peacock green Prismacolor marker; coated with epoxy
Eyes: Large gold Witchcraft eyes

Front view

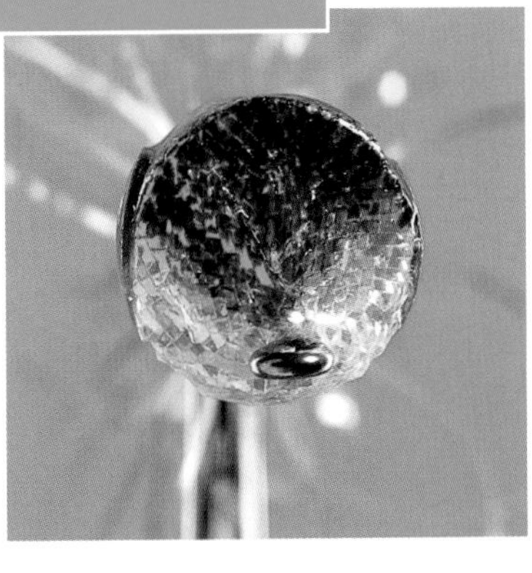

Benoit's Virtual Baitfish

Overall length: 4" on #2/0 hook
Pattern type: Baitfish
Primarily designed for: Striped bass
Submitted by: Eldredge Bros. Fly Shop (Cape Neddick, Maine)
Originated by: Brett Benoit
Tied by: Brett Benoit

Hook: Mustad 34011, #2/0
Thread: Chartreuse Flymaster Plus
Tail: 4 chartreuse saddle hackles veiled with pearl Flashabou
Body: 25-lb. monofilament over chartreuse thread
Ribbing: Grizzly saddle hackle, palmered
Wing: Chartreuse Streamer Hair
Belly: Chartreuse Streamer Hair
Eyes: Wapsi 3/16" red Hologram Eyes
Head: Epoxy over chartreuse thread

Blue Bird

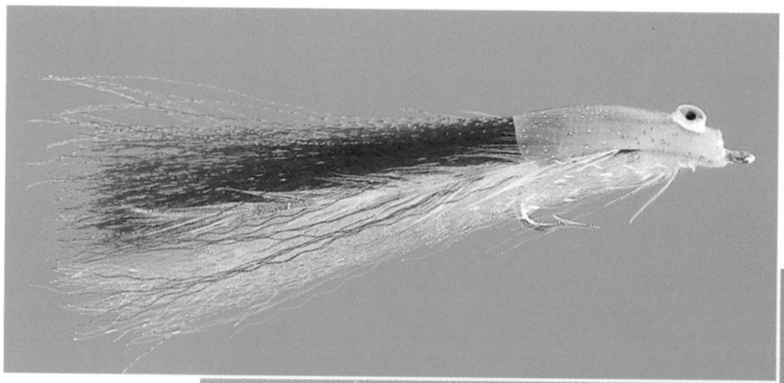

Top view

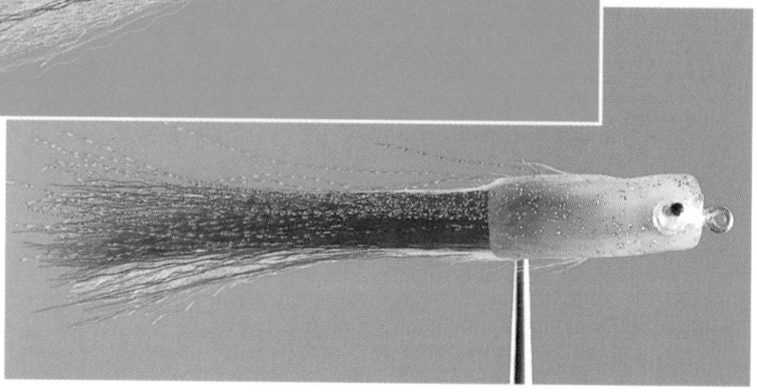

Overall length: 3 3/4" on #1 hook
Pattern type: General attractor
Primarily designed for: Bluefish
Also effective on: Striped bass
Submitted by: The Bear's Den Fly Fishing Shoppe (Taunton, Massachusetts)
Originated by: Thomas Martin
Tied by: Thomas Martin

Hook: Mustad 34007, #1
Thread: White
Wing: Blue Krystal Flash over blue Ultra Hair over white Ultra Hair, flanked by one narrow white saddle hackle on each side
Belly: White Ultra Hair
Shell: Synthetic fingernail, glued
Eyes: Google eye

Bow Tyer Arctic Fox Zonker

Overall length: 4 1/2" on #4/0 hook
Pattern type: General attractor
Primarily designed for: Striped bass
Submitted by: The Bear's Den Fly Fishing Shoppe (Taunton, Massachusetts)
Originated by: Herbert T. Cushman
Tied by: Herbert T. Cushman

Hook: Mustad 34011, #4/0
Thread: Red
Tail: Strip of chartreuse arctic fox fur
Body: Strip of chartreuse arctic fox fur, wrapped
Eyes: Aluminum barbell with plastic insert, red with black pupils

Clondas—Crafty Critter

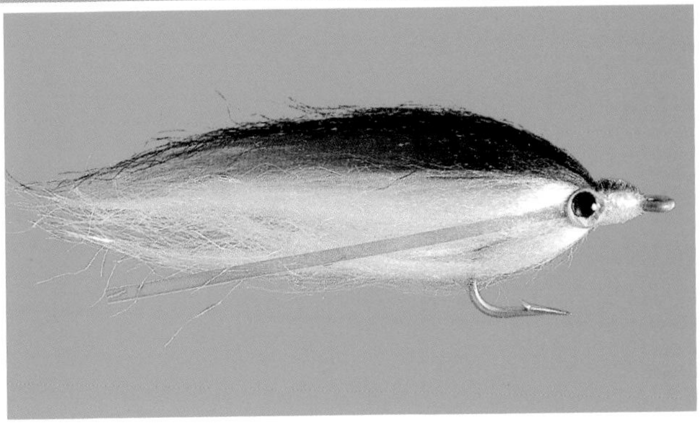

Overall length: 3" on #1 hook
Pattern type: Silverside or anchovy
Primarily designed for: Striped bass, bluefish
Also effective on: Bonito, Spanish mackerel
Submitted by: The Bear's Den Fly Fishing Shoppe (Taunton, Massachusetts)
Originated by: George Zissis Clondas
Tied by: George Zissis Clondas

Hook: Mustad 254SS, #1
Thread: Danville Fine Monofilament
Tail: Olive Comes Alive over White Kinky Fiber over pearl Polar Flash, surrounded on sides and bottom by white Comes Alive
Belly: White Comes Alive
Wing: Black Comes Alive over olive Comes Alive over white Comes Alive
Lateral line: Pearl Flashabou
Eyes: 3-D prismatic eyes, chartreuse with black pupils

Clondas—Kinky Angel

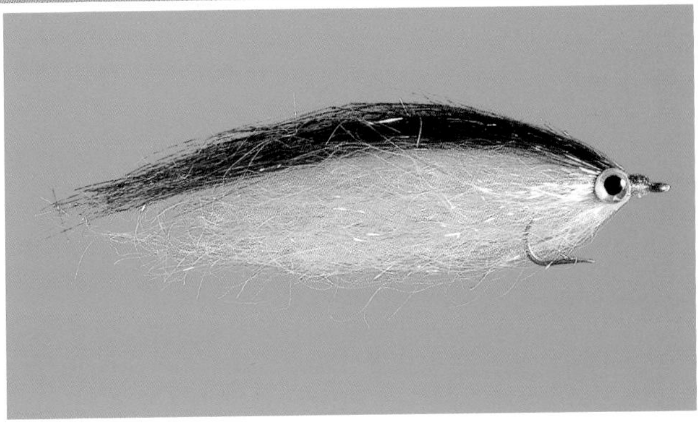

Overall length: 5" on #1/0 hook
Pattern type: Herring
Primarily designed for: Striped bass
Also effective on: Bluefish
Submitted by: The Bear's Den Fly Fishing Shoppe (Taunton, Massachusetts)
Originated by: George Zissis Clondas
Tied by: George Zissis Clondas

Hook: Mustad 254SS, #1/0 or larger
Thread: Danville Fine Monofilament
Tail: White Kinky Fiber
Belly: Pearl green Angel Hair over white Kinky Fiber
Wing: Baitfish Angel Hair over rainbow Angel Hair over blue Angel Hair
Eyes: 3-D Prismatic Eyes, glued

Double Bunny Clouser

Comments: This pattern combines Scott Sanchez's double-bunny style with the eyes of a Clouser Minnow. It can be tied in any number of color combinations, to imitate baitfish or to make an attractor pattern. The version shown here, says Bill Thompson, was his #1 striper fly for the season.

Overall length: 3 1/2" on #1 hook
Pattern type: General attractor
Primarily designed for: Striped bass
Also effective on: Bluefish
Submitted by: North Country Angler (Intervale, New Hampshire)
Originated by: Adaptation of Bob Clouser and Scott Sanchez design
Tied by: Bill Thompson

Hook: Standard shank saltwater, #1
Thread: White Monocord for body; fluorescent green Flymaster for head
Body: Bill's Body Braid
Wing: White rabbit fur strip over chartreuse rabbit fur strip, mounted behind hook eye; hide sides glued together, double-bunny style
Eyes: Barbell with Stick-on eyes

Emmons Bozo Herring

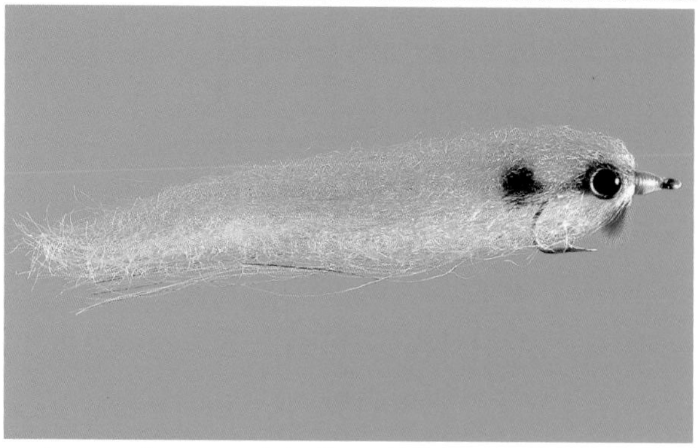

Overall length: 7 1/4" on #4/0 hook
Pattern type: Blueback herring
Primarily designed for: Striped bass
Also effective on: Bluefish
Submitted by: Eldredge Bros. Fly Shop (Cape Neddick, Maine)
Originated by: Bob Emmons
Tied by: Bob Emmons

Hook: Eagle Claw 254SS, #4/0; keel weighted with .035" non-toxic wire
Thread: White Flymaster Plus
Tail: White Bozo Hair colored with lime green Prismacolor marker over white Bozo Hair
Body: Pearl Body Braid colored on top with lime green Prismacolor marker
Wing: Light blue Bozo Hair over white Bozo hair colored with lime green Prismacolor marker; black spot added with black Prismacolor marker
Belly: White Bozo Hair over pearl Polar Flash
Throat: Red rabbit fur
Eyes: 10mm gold plastic eyes

Emmons Bozo Mackerel

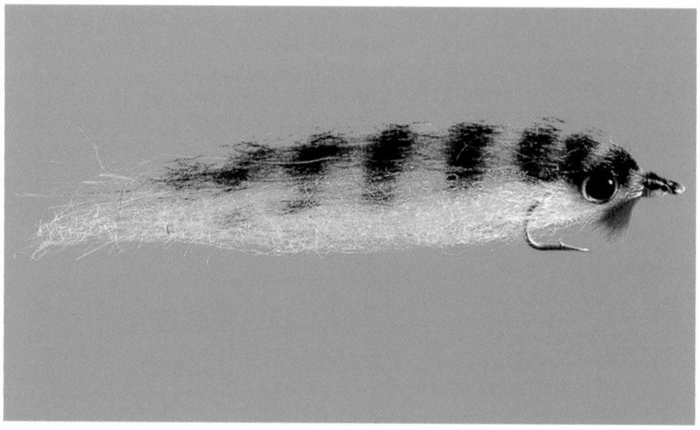

Overall length: 7" on #4/0 hook
Pattern type: Atlantic mackerel
Primarily designed for: Striped bass
Also effective on: Bluefish, jacks, yellowfin, dolphin
Submitted by: Eldredge Bros. Fly Shop (Cape Neddick, Maine)
Originated by: Bob Emmons
Tied by: Bob Emmons

Hook: Eagle Claw 254SS, #4/0; keel weighted with .035" non-toxic wire
Thread: White Flymaster Plus
Tail: White Bozo Hair colored with peacock blue Prismacolor marker, black stripes added with black marker, over white Bozo Hair
Body: Pearl E-Z Body Braid
Wing: White Bozo Hair colored with peacock blue Prismacolor marker, black stripes added with black marker, over pearl Fire Fly
Belly: White Bozo Hair over pearl Polar Flash
Throat: Red rabbit fur
Eyes: 10mm gold plastic eyes

Comments: Bob Emmons explains, "I originally designed this fly to imitate an Atlantic mackerel in a larger pattern, while making the fly easy to cast and durable. Bozo Hair has proven to be a great material for this fly. Being a synthetic, it does not hold water, so it's easy to cast, it maintains its silhouette in the water, it has a lot of action when fished, and gives the fly the appearance of depth because of the translucent properties of the materials. Special thanks to my friend Chris Henson for his advice while developing this fly."

Emmons Sandy Eel

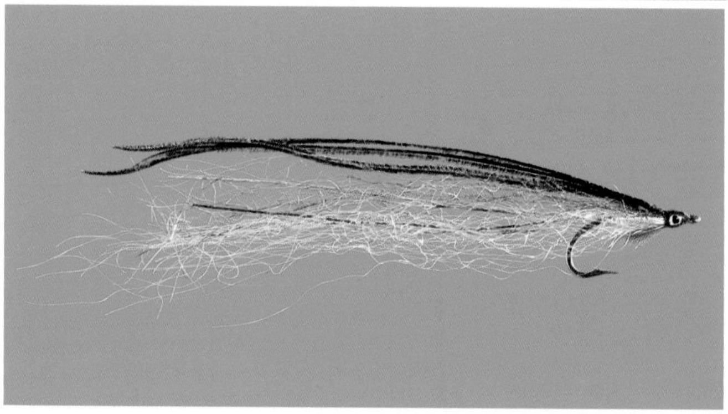

Overall length: 4 1/2" on #4 hook
Pattern type: Sand eel
Primarily designed for: Striped bass
Also effective on: Shad
Submitted by: Eldredge Bros. Fly Shop (Cape Neddick, Maine)
Originated by: Bob Emmons
Tied by: Bob Emmons

Hook: Mustad 34007, #4
Thread: Camel UNI 6/0
Body: Pearl Body Braid
Wing: Peacock herl over olive Bozo Hair over dark olive pearl Polar Flash
Belly: White Bozo Hair
Throat: Red rabbit fur
Eyes: Painted, white with black pupils

Comments: "This fly works best when tied very sparse," notes Bob Emmons. "I've had great luck fishing this fly on some of our beaches and estuaries."

Emmons Sea Worm

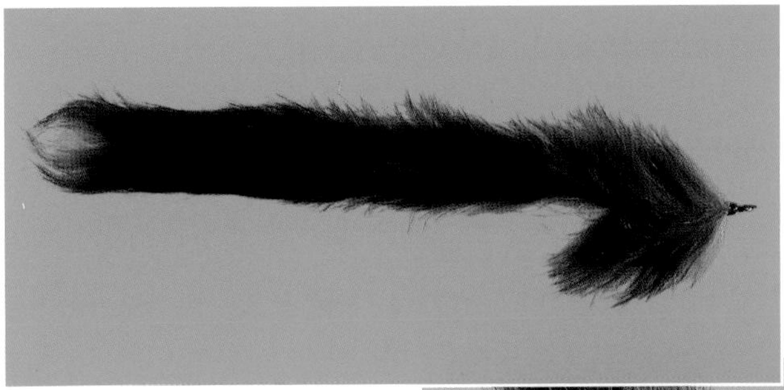

Overall length: 7 1/2" on #2/0 hook
Pattern type: Sea worm
Primarily designed for: Striped bass
Submitted by: Eldredge Bros. Fly Shop (Cape Neddick, Maine)
Originated by: Bob Emmons
Tied by: Bob Emmons

Hook: Mustad 34007, #2/0; shank wrapped with .020" non-toxic wire
Thread: Rusty brown UNI 6/0
Foul guard: Loop of 20-lb. Mason nylon
Tail: 2 crawfish orange Zonker strips, glued back-to-back with waterproof fabric glue
Body: Crawfish orange crosscut rabbit, wrapped
Pincers: 1 brown goose biot on each side of hook eye

Tail raised to show monofilament foul guard.

Emmons Silvery Sides

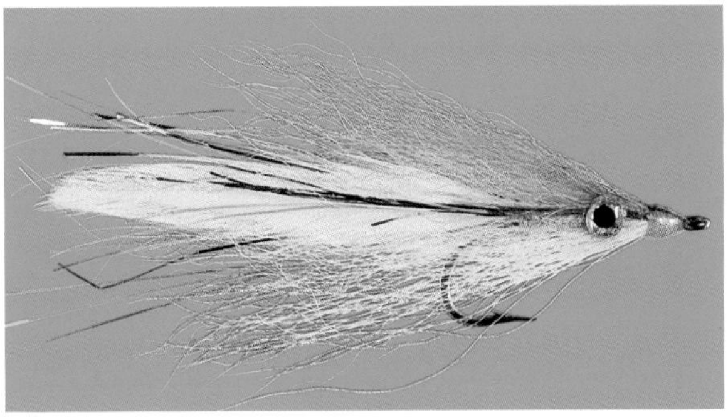

Overall length: 3 1/2" on #1/0 hook
Pattern type: Atlantic silversides
Primarily designed for: Striped bass
Submitted by: Eldredge Bros. Fly Shop (Cape Neddick, Maine)
Originated by: Bob Emmons
Tied by: Bob Emmons

Hook: Mustad 34007, #1/0
Thread: White UNI 6/0
Tail: 4 white saddle hackles
Body: Pearl E-Z Body, colored seafoam green on top with permanent marker
Belly: White bucktail, sparse
Wing: Brown bucktail dyed seafoam (from back of seafoam-dyed bucktail) over seafoam bucktail, both clumps 1/2 as thick as white used for belly
Lateral line: Salt and pepper Flashabou
Eyes: 1/8" silver Hologram Eyes

Comments: "This fly," notes Bob Emmons, "is fashioned after the style of the Lefty's Deceiver and has been extremely effective on our rivers and estuaries for striped bass."

Emmons Slippery Squid

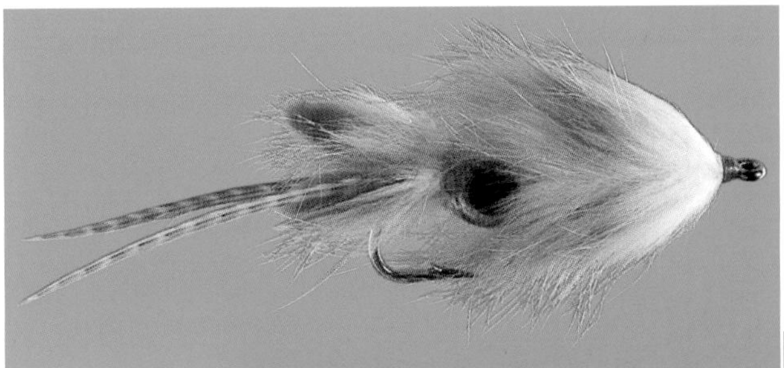

Overall length: 4" on #4/0 hook
Pattern type: Squid
Primarily designed for: Striped bass
Submitted by: Eldredge Bros. Fly Shop (Cape Neddick, Maine)
Originated by: Bob Emmons
Tied by: Bob Emmons

Hook: Mustad 34007, #4/0
Thread: Tan UNI 6/0
Long tentacles: 2 dark barred ginger hackles
Short tentacles: Light ginger hen hackles, surrounded by rabbit fur from body
Body: Light ginger crosscut rabbit strip, wrapped and trimmed close to shank in eye area
Eyes: 10mm gold plastic eyes, coated with epoxy

Bottom view

Comments: Bob Emmons notes that a small rubber band is used to hold the body fur forward while applying epoxy to the eyes and turning it to dry.

Emu Bucktail Herring

Overall length: 3 1/2" on #2/0 hook
Pattern type: Juvenile herring
Primarily designed for: Striped bass
Submitted by: Eldredge Bros. Fly Shop (Cape Neddick, Maine)
Originated by: Travis Johnson
Tied by: Travis Johnson

Hook: Mustad 34007, #2/0
Thread: White UNI 6/0
Tail: Seafoam green soft bucktail
Body: Pearl Body Braid
Wing: Peacock herl over seafoam green soft bucktail over 4 strands pearl Krystal Flash flanked by 1 emu feather per side
Belly: White soft bucktail, same quantity as used for tail and wing
Eyes: 3/16" Wapsi silver holographic eyes, glued on

Emu Herring Grocery Fly

Overall length: 7 1/2" on #4/0 hook
Pattern type: Adult herring or juvenile menhaden
Primarily designed for: Striped bass
Submitted by: Eldredge Bros. Fly Shop (Cape Neddick, Maine)
Originated by: Travis Johnson adaptation of Brock Apfel design
Tied by: Travis Johnson

Hook: Mustad 7766, #4/0; weighted with .025" lead wire
Thread: White Flymaster Plus
Tail: 2 white schlappen feathers flanked by 6 strands pearl Fire Fly
Body: Pearl Body Braid
Belly: White bucktail
Throat: Red rabbit fur
Lateral line: Pearl Krystal Flash
Wing: Peacock herl over white bucktail over 2 pairs seafoam green schlappen feathers over seafoam green bucktail, flanked by 1 medium black-tipped emu feather per side
Eyes: 5/16" silver holographic, glued on

First Light Loligo

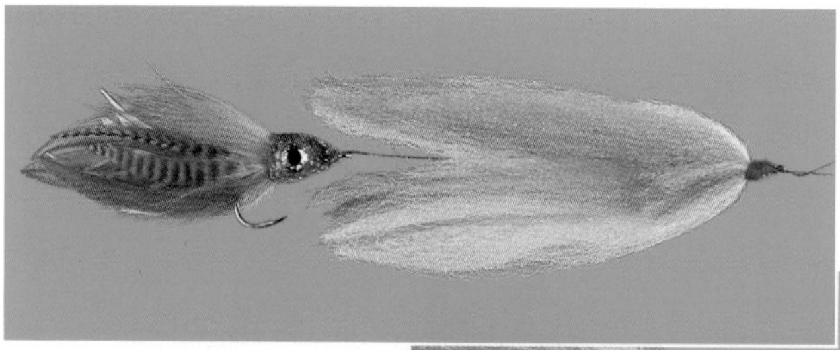

Detail of head.

Comments: Captain Nat Moody notes, "The wire body prevents bluefish bite off while remaining hidden from selective stripers. The best luck with this pattern has been along rocky shorelines as well as offshore rips. The fly can be fished with any retrieve, though a dead drift works especially well."

Overall length: 9 1/2" on #4/0 hook
Pattern type: North Atlantic squid
Primarily designed for: Striped bass, bluefish
Also effective on: School bluefin tuna
Submitted by: First Light Anglers (Manchester, Massachusetts)
Originated by: Captain Nat Moody
Tied by: Captain Nat Moody

Hook: Trey Combs Gamakatsu, #4/0; 42-lb. American Fishing Wire is snelled to hook and looped at head to form wire extension 6 1/2" long
Thread: Pink Danville Flymaster Plus, size A
Tentacles: Orange and ginger grizzly saddle hackles with white ostrich herl and pink marabou
Head: 1/2" E-Z Body tubing coated with 5-minute epoxy
Eyes: 1/4" silver 3D Eyes
Body: Pink, polar bear, orange, and red Near Hair, attached directly to wire and combed to blend

Flat Wing Deceiver (Herring)

Overall length: 6 3/4" on #6/0 hook
Pattern type: Adult herring
Primarily designed for: Striped bass, bluefish
Submitted by: The Bear's Den Fly Fishing Shoppe (Taunton, Massachusetts)
Originated by: Todd Kristofferson
Tied by: Todd Kristofferson

Hook: Gamakatsu Octopus or Owner Aki, #6/0-#2/0
Thread: 2-lb. clear monofilament
Tail: 2 long, white saddle hackles
Belly: White calf tail over red Krystal Flash over white bucktail
Wing: Peacock Lite Brite over olive bucktail over olive Fly Flash over white bucktail, flanked by pearl and silver Lite Brite
Eyes: Large molded holographic

Gee's Guitar Minnow (Bucktail)

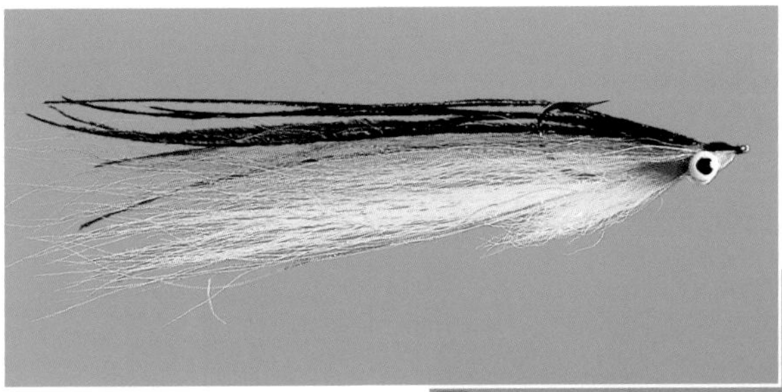

Bottom view, detail of gills.

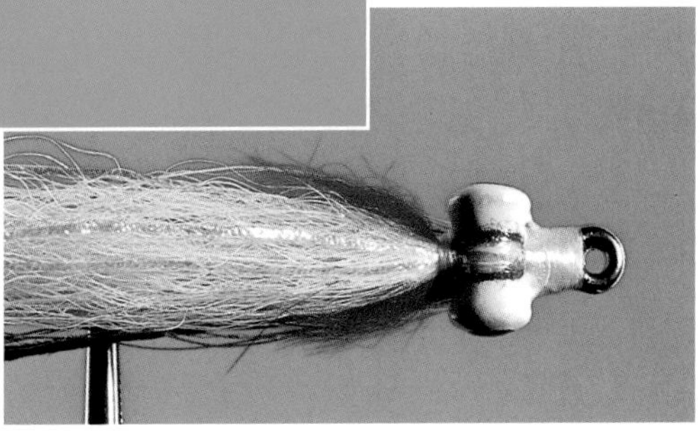

Overall length: 5 1/2" on #2/0 hook
Pattern type: Baby pollock, silversides, sand eel
Primarily designed for: Striped bass
Also effective on: Pollock, shad
Submitted by: Eldredge Bros. Fly Shop (Cape Neddick, Maine)
Originated by: Jim Bernstein adaptation of Bob Clouser design
Tied by: Jim Bernstein

Hook: Mustad 34007, #2/0
Thread: White UNI 6/0
Tail: White bucktail and 4-6 strands pearl Fire Fly Flash
Body: Bill Peabody's pearl Body Braid
Belly: White calf tail and pearl Fire Fly Flash
Gills: Red rabbit fur
Wing: Peacock herl over olive bucktail over seafoam green bucktail, flanked by pearl olive Krystal Flash
Eyes: Medium lead barbell eyes painted white with black pupils
Head: Black on top, colored with permanent marker

Gee's Guitar Minnow (Clouser)

Bottom view, detail of gills.

Overall length: 5 1/4" on #2/0 hook
Pattern type: Baby pollock, silversides, sand eel
Primarily designed for: Striped bass
Also effective on: Pollock, shad
Submitted by: Eldredge Bros. Fly Shop (Cape Neddick, Maine)
Originated by: Jim Bernstein adaptation of Bob Clouser design
Tied by: Jim Bernstein

Hook: Mustad 34007, #2/0
Thread: White UNI 6/0
Tail: 2-4 white saddle feathers flanked by 4-6 strands pearl Fire Fly
Body: Bill Peabody's Body Braid
Wing: Peacock herl over olive bucktail over seafoam green bucktail, flanked by pearl olive Krystal Flash
Belly: White calf tail (pearl Fire Fly optional)
Eyes: Medium lead barbell eyes, painted white with black pupils
Gills: Red rabbit fur
Head: Black on top, colored with permanent marker

Holy Mackerel Clouser

Overall length: 6" on #3/0 hook
Pattern type: Spike mackerel
Primarily designed for: Striped bass
Also effective on: Bluefish
Submitted by: Eldredge Bros. Fly Shop (Cape Neddick, Maine)
Originated by: Jim Bernstein adaptation of Bob Clouser design
Tied by: Jim Bernstein

Bottom view, detail of gills.

Hook: Partridge CS53, #3/0
Thread: White UNI 6/0
Tail: 2 white schlappen feathers and 6 strands pearl Fire Fly
Body: Bill Peabody's Body Braid
Wing: Behind eyes: yellow bucktail, flanked by 1 kingfisher blue saddle hackle per side, flanked by 1 highlander green saddle hackle per side. In front of eyes: peacock herl over highlander green bucktail
Belly: Pearl Fire Fly over white bucktail
Gills: Red rabbit fur
Eyes: 7/32" Spirit River Real Eyes
Head: Black on top, colored with permanent marker

Holy Mackerel Deceiver

Overall length: 6 1/4" on #3/0 hook
Pattern type: Mackerel
Primarily designed for: Striped bass
Also effective on: Bluefish
Submitted by: Maine Sport Outfitters (Rockport, Maine)
Originated by: Captain Forrest Faulkingham adaptation of Lefty's Deceiver
Tied by: Captain Forrest Faulkingham

Hook: Standard saltwater #2/0-#4/0
Thread: Gray 3/0 Monocord
Tail: Fountain Flashabou over 4 white schlappen feathers, butts over wrapped with silver Mylar tinsel
Belly: White bucktail flanked by gray bucktail on each side
Wing: Peacock herl over green bucktail flanked by one grizzly-dyed-green saddle feather per side, over fluorescent blue bucktail flanked by fluorescent blue/silver Krystal Flash
Gills: Red Krystal Flash
Eyes: 1/4" yellow plastic, glued on with Goop
Head: Tying thread coated with epoxy

Comments: Captain Forrest Faulkingham notes, "This has been an extremely effective pattern on the Maine coast. We fish this in the surf and around ledges and sand bars in turbulent water."

Jim's Grocery Mackerel

Overall length: 8" on #5/0 hook
Pattern type: Tinker mackerel
Primarily designed for: Striped bass
Also effective on: Bluefish
Submitted by: Eldredge Bros. Fly Shop (Cape Neddick, Maine)
Originated by: Jim Bernstein adaptation of Brock Apfel design
Tied by: Jim Bernstein

Hook: Mustad 7766 or TMC 800S, #5/0; weighted with 9" of .030" lead wire
Thread: White Flymaster Plus
Tail: 4 white schlappen feathers and 8 strands pearl Fire Fly
Body: Bill Peabody's Body Braid
Belly: White bucktail
Throat: Red rabbit fur
Wing: Peacock herl over green bucktail (striped with black marker), flanked by 1 green grizzly saddle hackle per side
Lateral line (optional): Green Krystal Flash
Eyes: 10mm gold plastic eyes

Jim's Grocery Pollock

Overall length: 6 1/4" on #4/0 hook
Pattern type: Pollock
Primarily designed for: Striped bass
Submitted by: Eldredge Bros. Fly Shop (Cape Neddick, Maine)
Originated by: Jim Bernstein adaptation of Brock Apfel design
Tied by: Jim Bernstein
Hook: Mustad 7766 or TMC 800S, #4/0; weighted with 9" of .025" lead wire
Thread: White Flymaster Plus
Tail: 1 white schlappen feather per side, flanked by 1 seafoam schlappen per side, flanked by 8 strands pearl Fire Fly Flash
Body: Bill Peabody's pearl Body Braid
Belly: White bucktail
Throat: Red rabbit fur
Wing: Peacock herl over olive bucktail over 2 olive schlappen feathers over seafoam bucktail, flanked by 1 emu feather and 6 strands copper Flashabou per side
Eyes: 7/32" gold plastic eyes
Head: Colored black on top with permanent marker

Comments: Jim Bernstein explains, "My inspiration for this fly came from long conversations with Bill Catherwood and Art Swanson. Bill introduced me to emu as a tying material. This has been my best pattern for consistently catching large stripers on the southern Maine coast."

Lunch

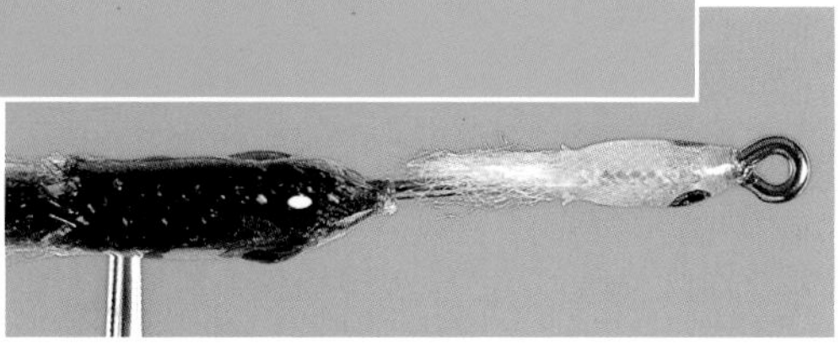

Top view

Overall length: 5 1/4" on #3/0 hook
Pattern type: Juvenile mackerel chasing silverside
Primarily designed for: Striped bass
Submitted by: Maine Sport Outfitters (Rockport, Maine)
Originated by: Captain Forrest Faulkingham
Tied by: Captain Forrest Faulkingham
Hook: Mustad 34011, #3/0
Thread: Monofilament
Mackerel wing: Black Craft Fur over olive Polafibre over white Polafibre, tied on 195-lb. stainless wire as explained below
Lateral line: Holographic Angel Hair
Mackerel body: Large pearl E-Z Body, colored on top with olive permanent marker, coated with epoxy
Gills: Red permanent marker
Mackerel eyes: 1/4" yellow Stick-on eyes
Silverside body: Small pearl Mylar braid over white Polafibre, coated with epoxy
Silverside eyes: #2 gold eyes

Comments: In this unique dressing technique, the mackerel wing and lateral line are dressed on a 3" length of 195-lb. stainless wire. When complete, pierce a length of E-Z Body tubing with the hook and move the braid down the hook bend. Insert the completed mackerel body through the rear of the body braid. Slide this assembly up the bend and 1/3 of the way to eye of the hook. Tie down the front of the E-Z Body and cement it. Use a pair of pliers to pull out the stainless wire. Arrange the body braid as shown in the photograph—primarily above and parallel to the shank. Apply eyes, gills, and 2 coats of epoxy; warming the epoxy gives better results. The silverside portion is dressed by sliding the body tubing over Polafibre attached to the shank. Add eyes and coat with epoxy.

Peacock Eel

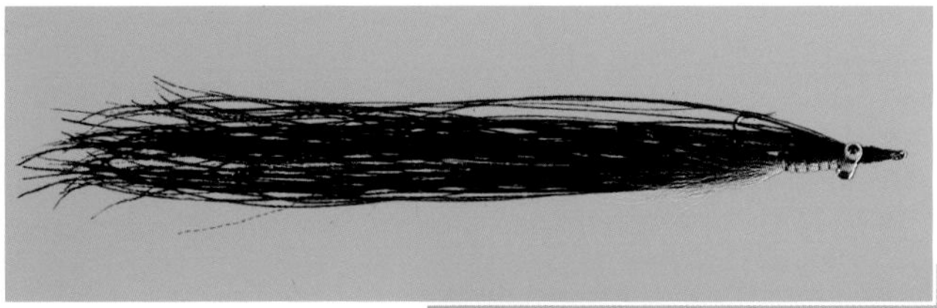

Detail of head and belly.

Overall length: 11 1/2" on #4/0 hook
Pattern type: Eel
Primarily designed for: Striped bass
Submitted by: Eldredge Bros. Fly Shop (Cape Neddick, Maine)
Originated by: Jim Bernstein
Tied by: Jim Bernstein
Hook: Mustad 34011, #4/0; weighted with 3" of wrapped .025" lead wire
Thread: Black Flymaster Plus
Tail: Peacock herl and black Krystal Flash
Body: Peacock herl
Belly: White bucktail, colored yellow on sides with marker, coated with cement after ribbing
Ribbing: Medium copper wire, counterwrapped
Wing: Peacock herl
Eyes: 7/32" Spirit River Real Eyes
Head: Peacock herl

Pola-Herring

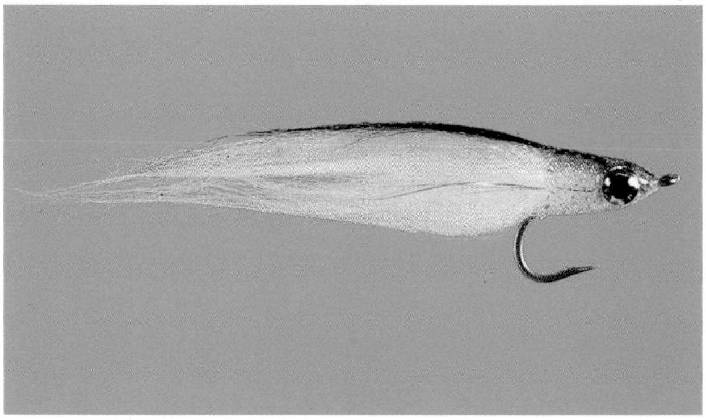

Overall length: 4 1/2" on #1/0 hook
Pattern type: Young herring
Primarily designed for: Striped bass
Submitted by: Maine Sport Outfitters (Rockport, Maine)
Originated by: Captain Forrest Faulkingham
Tied by: Captain Forrest Faulkingham

Hook: Short shank, #1/0
Thread: Monofilament
Wing: Black Craft Fur over lavender Polafibre over white Polafibre
Lateral line: Holographic Angel Hair
Body: Large pearl E-Z Body, coated with 5-minute epoxy
Eyes: 1/4" silver Stick-on eyes

Comments: Captain Forrest Faulkingham notes that this fly has good movement is especially effective in clear, calm water.

Rhody Flat-Wing

Overall length: 4 1/2" on #2/0 hook
Pattern type: General attractor
Primarily designed for: Striped bass
Also effective on: Bluefish, weakfish, and bonito
Submitted by: North Country Angler (Intervale, New Hampshire)
Originated by: Bill Peabody
Tied by: Bill Thompson

Hook: Standard shank saltwater hook, #2/0
Thread: White Monocord
Tail: Coarse white bucktail distributed around shank, flanked with holographic Flashabou, topped with one white schlappen hackle
Body: Bill's Body Braid or pearl Mylar
Collar: White bucktail
Wing: Peacock herl over pearl Crystal Hair over white bucktail

Comments: This fly, says Bill Thompson, was first tied by Bill Peabody of Portsmouth, Rhode Island, "one of the great tyers of saltwater flies on the East Coast."

Rick's Murky Deceiver

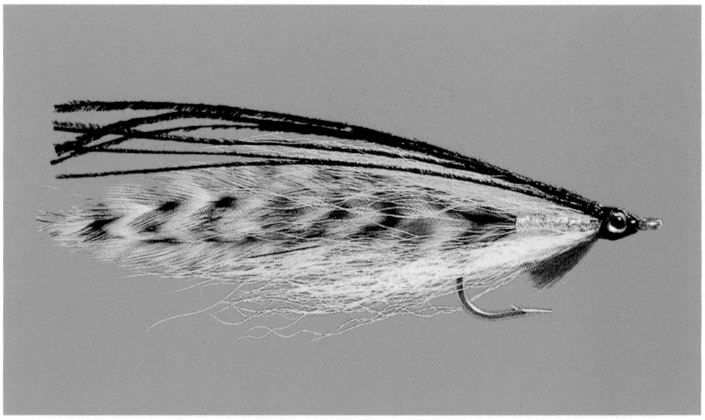

Overall length: 3 3/4" on #1/0 hook
Pattern type: Attractor, sand eel, silverside
Primarily designed for: Striped bass
Also effective on: Bluefish
Submitted by: Eldredge Bros. Fly Shop (Cape Neddick, Maine)
Originated by: Rick Sharp version of Lefty Kreh Deceiver
Tied by: Rick Sharp

Hook: TMC 800S, #1/0
Thread: Danville Fine Monofilament
Tail: Pale olive pearl Polar Flash over chartreuse bucktail flanked by 2 chartreuse grizzly hackles per side
Body: Flat pearl braid body wrap
Belly: Yellow bucktail
Throat: Fluorescent red SLF hank
Wing: Peacock herl over chartreuse bucktail
Eyes: Witchcraft clear 3mm eyes

Comments: Rick Sharp explains, "Though designed for spring runoff conditions on the Merrimack River, this fly is effective year round, especially when there are lots of naturals in the water and you need something to stand out. It's a good alternative to using a Clouser, especially when guiding clients new to the sport. It's easy to cast and effective with a line like the Teeny 250. Note that the use of the red throat is important."

Scott's Shrimp

Overall length: 1 1/2" on #1/0 hook
Pattern type: Shrimp
Primarily designed for: Striped bass
Also effective on: Sea-run brown trout, bonefish, permit
Submitted by: The Bear's Den Fly Fishing Shoppe (Taunton, Massachusetts)
Originated by: Kevin Donahue
Tied by: Kevin Donahue

Hook: Mustad 34007, #1/0; weighted with lead wire wrapped around shank
Thread: Brown 6/0
Antennae: Brown hackle fibers mixed with pearl Krystal Flash
Eyes: 100-lb. monofilament, melted, ends blackened with permanent marker
Body: Brown hackles
Shellback: Clear plastic strip, 1" long and 1/4" wide
Ribbing: 10-lb. mono
Tail: Hackle tips from body

Comments: After mounting antennae and eyes, wrap shank with lead. Attach hackles by the tips, leaving tips extending out over hook eye. Wrap hackles back to bend; trim away hackle fibers on top of body. Fold shellback over body and secure with mono ribbing.

Sea Hag (Clouser)

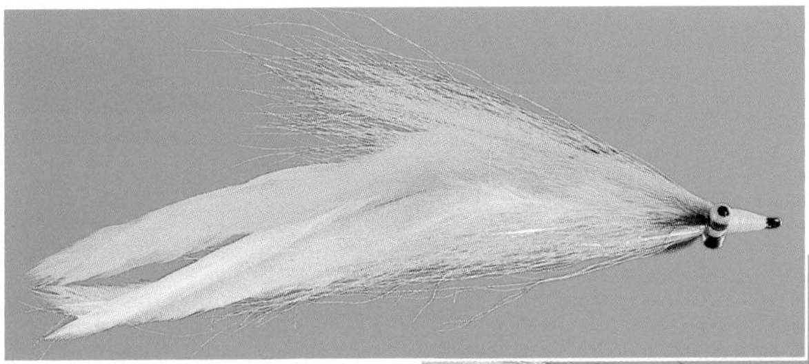

Overall length: 7 3/4" on #4/0 hook
Pattern type: Attractor
Primarily designed for: Striped bass
Also effective on: Bluefish
Submitted by: Eldredge Bros. Fly Shop (Cape Neddick, Maine)
Originated by: Jim Bernstein adaptation of Bob Clouser design
Tied by: Jim Bernstein

Bottom view, detail of gills.

Hook: Mustad 34011, #4/0; weighted with 5" of .020" lead wire
Thread: White Flymaster Plus
Tail: Pearl Fire Fly over white bucktail, flanked by 2 white schlappen feathers per side
Body: Rear half: Bill Peabody's Body Braid; front half: chartreuse UNI-Stretch
Wing: Behind eyes: chartreuse bucktail flanked by 1 chartreuse schlappen feather per side.
In front of eyes: chartreuse bucktail
Belly: Pearl Fire Fly over white bucktail
Gills: Red rabbit fur
Eyes: 1/4" Spirit River Real Eyes
Head: Chartreuse UNI-Stretch

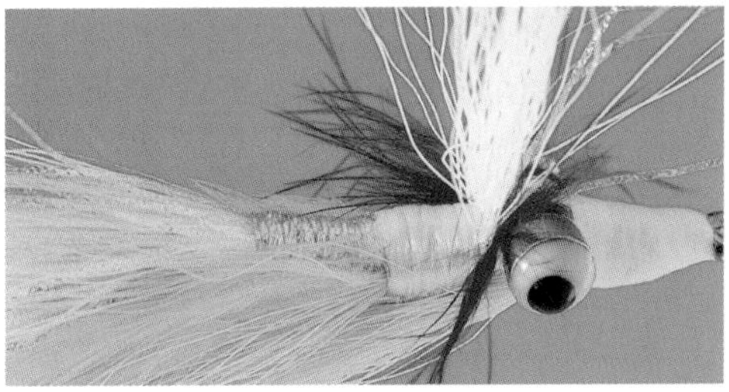

Here, the white belly hair has been raised to show the placement of body, belly, and wing materials.

Searsport Sand Eel

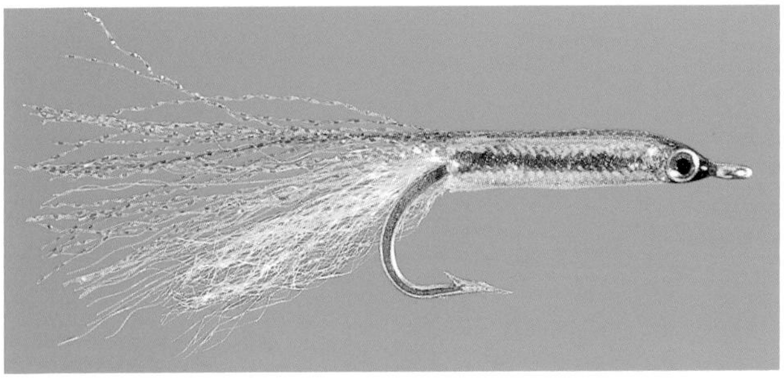

Overall length: 2 1/2" on #1/0 hook
Pattern type: Sand eel
Primarily designed for: Striped bass
Submitted by: Thom's of Maine (Houlton, Maine)
Originated by: Thom Willard
Tied by: Thom Willard

Hook: Mustad 34007, #1/0
Thread: Black UNI 6/0
Body: 10 strands purple Krystal Flash over 10 strands smoke Super Hair over white Polar Aire; wrap hook shank with olive UNI-Stretch; slide length of pearlescent Mylar tubing over shank and secure behind eye with olive UNI-Stretch to form head.
Wing: Tie in 10 strands peacock Krystal Flash behind hook eye. Then coat body and wing to hook bend with Devcon 5-minute epoxy
Eyes: Silver holographic Stick-on eyes

Comments: This pattern is used for striped bass along the Maine coast and Penobscot Bay and river.

Searun Muddler

Top view

Overall length: 1 1/4" on #6 hook
Pattern type: Mumichog
Primarily designed for: Sea-run brown and brook trout
Also effective on: Striped bass
Submitted by: Eldredge Bros. Fly Shop (Cape Neddick, Maine)
Originated by: Mark Drummond version of Don Gapen Muddler Minnow
Tied by: Mark Drummond

Hook: 4XL, #2-#8
Thread: Olive
Body: 4 strands olive Krystal Flash, wrapped
Underwing: Tag ends of Krystal Flash from body, folded back and tied in position
Wing: Olive grizzly marabou
Collar: Tips from deer hair head
Head: Olive deer hair, spun and clipped
Eyes: Small yellow-and-black eyes, glued on with Goop

Sharp's Baby Herring

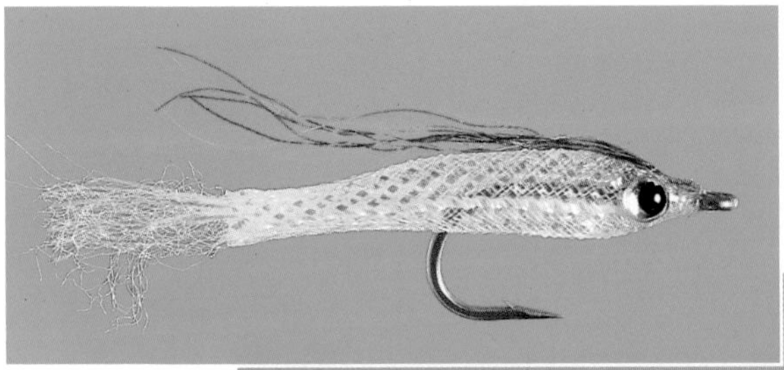

Top view

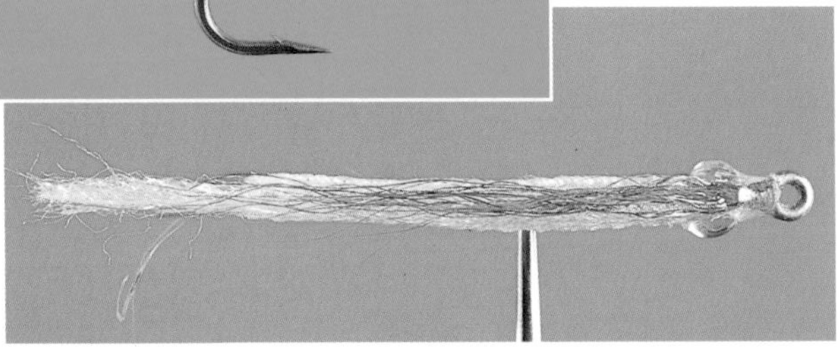

Overall length: 2 3/4" on #1/0 hook
Pattern type: Juvenile herring
Primarily designed for: Striped bass
Also effective on: Bluefish
Submitted by: Eldredge Bros. Fly Shop (Cape Neddick, Maine)
Originated by: Rick Sharp
Tied by: Rick Sharp

Hook: TMC 800S, #1/0
Thread: Danville Fine Monofilament
Tail: Bestway Near Hair (polar bear) with a few strands Tiewell rainbow pearl Sparkle Flash
Body: Medium pearl E-Z Body Braid
Wing: Teal bucktail over dark green bucktail over red bucktail, sparse
Eyes: 3mm Witchcraft clear

Comments: Tyer Rich Sharp notes that this fly was developed in the Lobsterville parking lot while waiting for the evening tide. To dress the fly, flatten a 2-inch piece of E-Z Body Braid by pinching between thumb and forefinger of both hands, pushing the material together lengthwise while squeezing with the fingers. Insert the hook through the braid. Use a bobbin threader to pull tail material through braid; secure tailing fibers behind hook eye. Secure braid behind hook eye. Put a few drops Flexament or Zap-A-Gap at tail end of braid, then pinch end of braid and push forward to create wrist at tail. After attaching wing and eyes, epoxy the fly head. Run some epoxy over the belly ridge of the fly to help maintain the flattened shape.

Silverside Deceiver

Overall length: 4" on #1 hook
Pattern type: Silversides
Primarily designed for: Striped bass
Also effective on: Bluefish
Submitted by: Eldredge Bros. Fly Shop (Cape Neddick, Maine)
Originated by: Mark Drummond version of Lefty Kreh Deceiver
Tied by: Mark Drummond

Hook: Saltwater, #1/0-#2
Thread: White
Tail: 4-6 gray saddle hackles
Body: Pearl Mylar tubing, secured only behind hook eye, then frayed to form collar beneath belly and wing; collar trimmed even with base of tail
Belly: White bucktail
Wing: Gray ghost Krystal Flash over gray bucktail
Lateral line: Gray Fire Fly
Eyes: Painted, white with black pupils

Softex Squid

Overall length: 4 1/4" on #4/0 hook
Pattern type: Squid
Primarily designed for: Striped bass
Also effective on: Bluefish
Submitted by: The Bear's Den Fly Fishing Shoppe (Taunton, Massachusetts)
Originated by: Scott Wessels
Tied by: Scott Wessels

Hook: Mustad 34007, #4/0
Thread: White Flat waxed nylon
Tail: White ostrich herl over pearl Glimmer over one white saddle hackle dipped in Softex, flanked by one white saddle hackle on each side
Collar: White marabou
Body: 5/16" opal tubing, sleeved inside itself to make a double layer, dipped in Softex
Eyes: 5/16" pearl prismatic Stick-on eyes

Walsh Schoolie

Top view

Overall length: 3" on #2/0 hook
Pattern type: Silversides, sand eel
Primarily designed for: Striped bass
Submitted by: The Fly Fisherman's Place (Thomaston, Maine)
Originated by: Terry Walsh
Tied by: Terry Walsh

Hook: Mustad 34011, #2/0
Thread: White; red thread for wing tie-down at rear and gill band behind eyes
Tail: White bucktail bound along entire length of shank
Body: 3/16" Universal Vise Corp. opal tubing
Wing: Peacock herl over white bucktail
Eyes: 1/8" Stick-on eyes

Walshie's Striper Fly

Overall length: 2 3/4" on #1/0 hook
Pattern type: Baitfish
Primarily designed for: Striped bass
Submitted by: Maine Sport Outfitters (Rockport, Maine)
Originated by: Terry Walsh
Tied by: Terry Walsh

Hook: Mustad 34007, #1/0
Thread: White 3/0
Tail: White bucktail
Wing: Peacock herl over chartreuse bucktail over white bucktail
Lateral line: Dark blue turkey quill segment
Throat: Red hackle fibers
Cheek: Barred teal
Eyes: Witchcraft Lure Eye, 4mm
Head: Easy Shape Sparkle Body

Wool-Head Deceiver

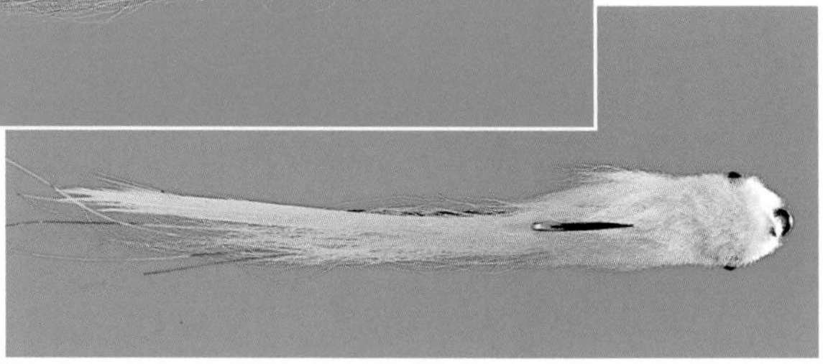

Top view

Comments: Like the original Deceiver, this version can be tied in any combination of colors and sizes.

Overall length: 5″ on #3/0 hook
Pattern type: Attractor, general baitfish
Primarily designed for: Striped bass
Also effective on: Bluefish
Submitted by: Eldredge Bros. Fly Shop (Cape Neddick, Maine)
Originated by: Dave Beattie adaptation of Lefty Kreh Deceiver
Tied by: Captain Dave Beattie

Hook: TMC 800S or Mustad 34007, #3/0
Thread: Any strong white thread or color to match head wool
Tail: 4-6 white saddle hackles flanked with pearl Mylar, and 1 thin grizzly hackle per side
Body: Pearl wrap
Belly: Any long white hair with good action
Wing: Any long white hair with good action
Eyes: 7/32″ barbell eyes tied just forward of mid-shank
Collar: Tips of head wool left long
Head: White wool, stacked and clipped to shape

CHAPTER 2

Mid-Atlantic States

Connecticut – Maryland – New Jersey New York – Pennsylvania – Virginia

A.J.F. Back Bend (Herring)

Overall length: 4 1/2" on #3/0 hook
Pattern type: Herring
Primarily designed for: Striped bass, bluefish
Also effective on: Weakfish
Submitted by: The Camp-Site (Huntington Station, New York)
Originated by: Amedeo J. Forzano
Tied by: Amedeo J. Forzano

Hook: Mustad 3407SS or Daiichi X Point, #3/0; bent 30 degrees away from hook point behind hook eye, bendback style
Thread: White 6/0
Wing: Peacock Krystal Flash over purple bucktail over pink bucktail over pink Krystal Flash over white bucktail
Head: Red Krystal Flash, wrapped
Eyes: Witchcraft Stick-on eyes, silver with black pupils; head and eyes coated with epoxy

Albie Slider

Overall length: 4" on #1 hook
Pattern type: Wounded baitfish
Primarily designed for: False albacore, bonito

Also effective on: Striped bass, bluefish
Submitted by: The Fly Hatch (Shrewsbury, New Jersey)
Originated by: Captain Dave Chouinard
Tied by: David Frassinelli

Bottom view

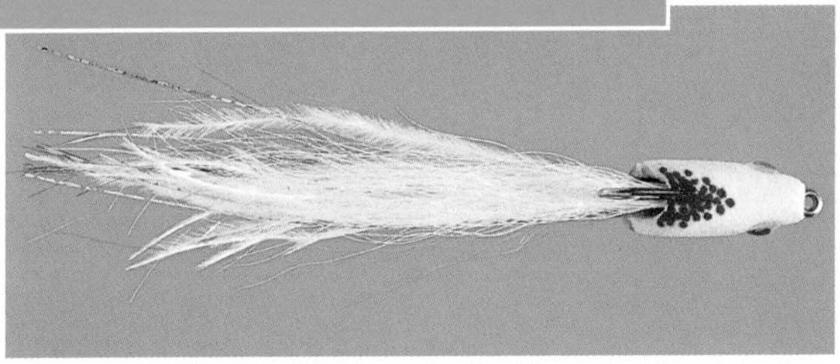

Hook: Mustad 34007, #1/0-#2
Thread: White 3/0
Tail: Olive Lite Brite over olive bucktail over silver Holographic Flash over few strands pearl Lite Brite over 20 strands white ostrich herl over sparse clump white bucktail
Head: #2 EdgeWater Stretch Composite, cut at 45-degree angle at rear and hollowed out, colored as shown with Pantone markers
Eyes: Prismatic Stick-on eyes

Comments: This fly is fished on a floating line and retrieved slowly, in short strips.

Amedeo's Bluefish Squid

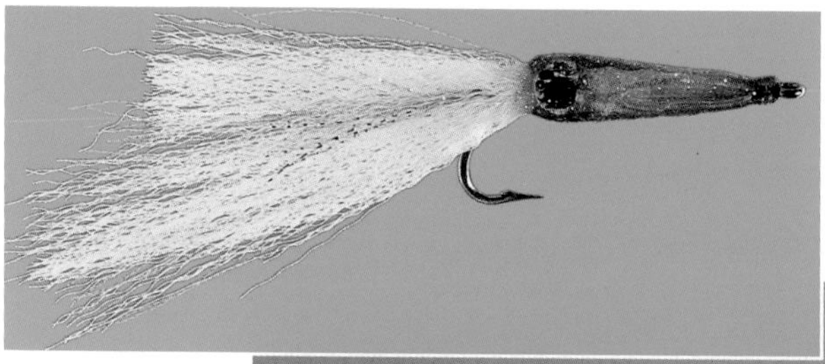

Top view

Overall length: 4" on #3/0 hook
Pattern type: Squid
Primarily designed for: Bluefish, striped bass
Also effective on: Weakfish
Submitted by: The Camp-Site (Huntington Station, New York)
Originated by: Amedeo J. Forzano
Tied by: Amedeo J. Forzano

Hook: Saltwater, #4/0-#2/0
Thread: Clear monofilament
Tentacles: Shorter bunch of white Ultra Hair over rainbow Krystal Flash over longer bunch of white Ultra Hair mixed with pearl Krystal Flash
Back: Purple Krystal Flash
Belly: Purple Krystal Flash
Tail: 2 pieces Witchcraft Mylar tape, cut to shape and sandwiched around hook shank
Body: 5-minute epoxy
Eyes: Witchcraft Stick-on eyes, silver holographic with black pupils

Comments: To form the body, mount the back and belly materials atop the wrapped butts of the tentacles materials. Pull back and belly materials forward, shellback style, and secure behind hook eye. Because tentacle butts are thick, the back and belly materials will not lie against the hook shank, but form an open "frame" that is filled with epoxy. The epoxy is built up in coats to cover back and belly materials, tail, and eyes.

Amedeo's Epoxy Squid

Bottom view

Overall length: 6 1/2" on #2/0 hook
Pattern type: Squid
Primarily designed for: Striped bass
Also effective on: Bluefish, weakfish
Submitted by: The Camp-Site (Huntington Station, New York)
Originated by: Amedeo J. Forzano
Tied by: Amedeo J. Forzano

Hook: Mustad 34011, #4/0-#2/0
Thread: Clear monofilament
Tentacles: White Ultra Hair over lavender Ultra Hair, mixed with pearl Krystal Flash; flanked by 8-10 white saddle hackles, 2 tied longer than the rest
Back: Purple Ultra Hair and pearl Krystal Flash
Belly: Purple Ultra Hair
Tail: 2 pieces Witchcraft Mylar tape cut to shape, sandwiched around hook shank and belly material
Body: 5-minute epoxy
Eyes: Witchcraft Stick-on eyes, silver holographic with black pupils

Comments: This pattern is most effective in purple, black, and pink. For details of tail construction, see supplementary photo and "Comments" under "Amedeo's Bluefish Squid," above.

Amedeo's Glow in the Dark

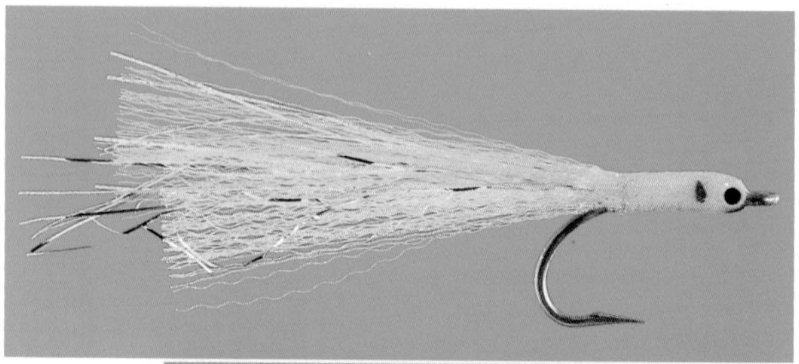

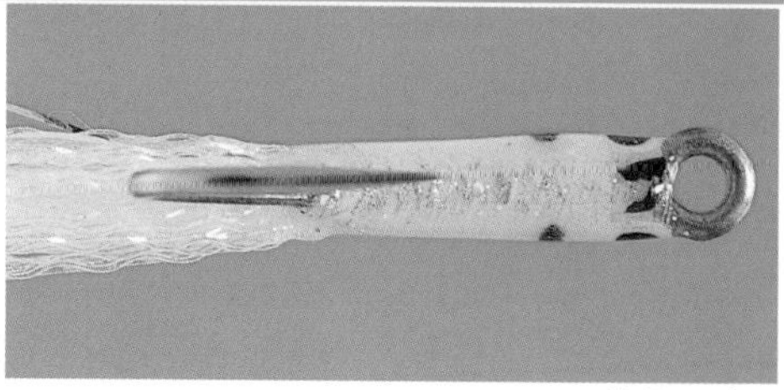

Bottom view

Overall length: 3" on #1 hook
Pattern type: Baitfish
Primarily designed for: Striped bass
Also effective on: Bluefish, false albacore, bonito
Submitted by: The Camp-Site (Huntington Station, New York)
Originated by: Amedeo J. Forzano
Tied by: Amedeo J. Forzano

Hook: Eagle Claw 254SS, #1
Thread: Clear monofilament
Wing: Neon green Ultra Hair over silver Flashabou mixed with a few strands of glow-in-the-dark Mylar, over polar bear Ultra Hair; all attached behind hook eye
Body: Silver Mylar braid wrapped around shank; wing hair pulled over top shellback style; all coated with 5-minute epoxy mixed with Witchcraft glow powder
Eyes: Witchcraft Stick-on eyes, green with black pupils
Gills and throat: Red permanent marker

Andy's 'Cuda Magnet

Overall length: 3 1/4" on #1/0 hook
Pattern type: Attractor
Primarily designed for: Barracuda
Submitted by: The Fly Fishing Shop (Far Hills, New Jersey)
Originated by: Andy Sutton
Tied by: Andy Sutton

Hook: Mustad 34011, #1/0
Thread: Fine Translucent
Tail: Pearl Krystal Flash over polar bear Ultra Hair, topped with neon green Ultra Hair from shellback
Underbody: Pearlescent Mylar
Overbody: Silver flake Jelly Cord
Shellback: Neon green (or hot pink or neon yellow) Ultra Hair
Eyes: 3/16" silver prism
Bill: Green (or pink or yellow) UNI-Stretch

Andy's Glow Squid

Top view

Overall length: 5" on 3/0 hook
Pattern type: Squid
Primarily designed for: Striped bass, bluefish
Submitted by: The Fly Fishing Shop (Far Hills, New Jersey)
Originated by: Andy Sutton
Tied by: Andy Sutton

Hook: Mustad 34011, #3/0
Thread: Fine Translucent
Mouth: 3 turns black suede cord
Tentacles: 2 strips 1/8" pearlescent (or chartreuse) tinsel; 8 strands white (or tan or chartreuse) suede cord
Body: Phosphorescent Rexlace
Mantle: White (or tan, or chartreuse) Near Hair dotted with phosphorescent fabric paint
Eyes: 5/16" phosphorescent Stick-on eyes

Andy's Grass Shrimp

Overall length: 1 1/2" on #4 hook
Pattern type: Grass shrimp
Primarily designed for: Striped bass, weakfish
Also effective on: Bonefish, white perch
Submitted by: The Fly Fishing Shop (Far Hills, New Jersey)
Originated by: Andy Sutton
Tied by: Andy Sutton

Hook: Mustad 34007, #2-#6
Thread: Ultra Fine Translucent
Antennae: Tan Super Hair (or olive, white, chartreuse, yellow, or brown for other versions)
Eyes: Small black or olive mono barbell eyes
Body: Tan Estaz (or olive, pearl, chartreuse, yellow, or root beer for other versions)
Shellback: Tan Neer Hair (or olive, white, chartreuse, yellow, or brown for other versions)

Andy's Rain Fish

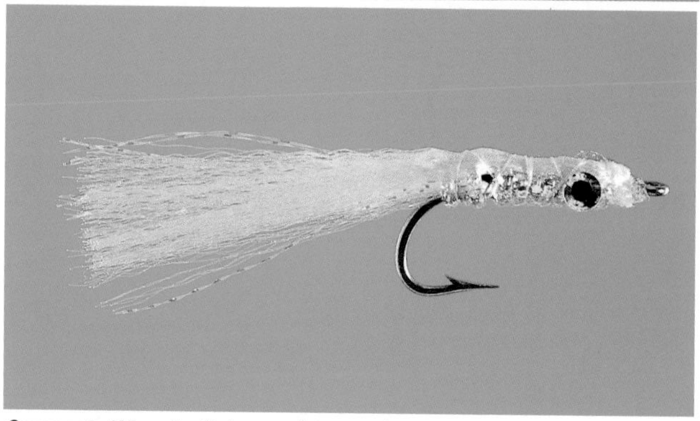

Overall length: 2 1/4" on #2 hook
Pattern type: Rain fish (bay anchovy)
Primarily designed for: Striped bass, bluefish
Also effective on: False albacore
Submitted by: The Fly Fishing Shop (Far Hills, New Jersey)
Originated by: Andy Sutton
Tied by: Andy Sutton

Hook: Mustad 34007, #2
Thread: Fine Translucent thread
Tail: Clear Super Hair flanked by pearl Krystal Flash
Underbody: Silver Mylar tinsel
Overbody: Silver flake Jelly Cord
Shellback: Light tan (or chartreuse) Super Hair or Ultra Hair, extending to tip of tail
Eyes: 5/32" silver prism Stick-on eyes

Comments: When the fly is complete, coat head, eyes, and shellback with Loon Hard Head.

Andy's Sand Eel

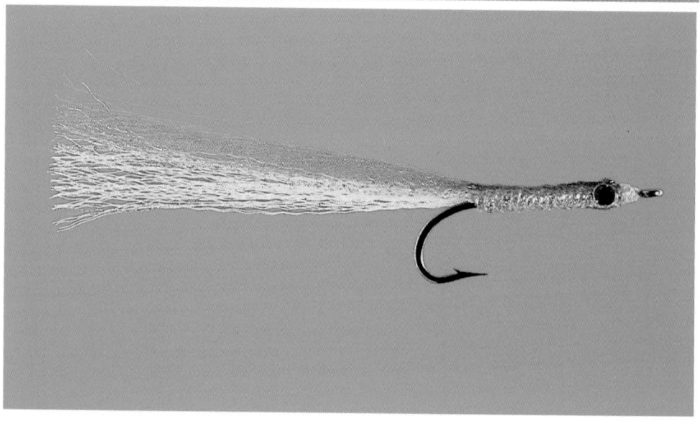

Overall length: 4 1/4" on #1/0 hook
Pattern type: Sand eel
Primarily designed for: Striped bass, bluefish
Submitted by: The Fly Fishing Shop (Far Hills, New Jersey)
Originated by: Andy Sutton
Tied by: Andy Sutton

Hook: Mustad 34011, #1/0
Thread: Fine Translucent thread
Tail: White Ultra Hair flanked by pearl Krystal Flash
Underbody: Pearlescent Mylar tinsel
Overbody: Silver flake Jelly Cord
Shellback: Olive (or chartreuse, blue, lavender, or black) Super Hair or Ultra Hair, extending to tip of tail
Eyes: 5/32" silver prism Stick-on eyes

Comments: When the fly is complete, coat head, eyes, and shellback with Loon Hard Head.

Andy's Sand Flea

Overall length: 1 1/2" on #4 hook
Pattern type: Sand flea
Primarily designed for: Striped bass
Submitted by: The Fly Fishing Shop (Far Hills, New Jersey)
Originated by: Andy Sutton adaptation of Brian Horsley pattern
Tied by: Andy Sutton

Hook: Mustad 34007, #4
Thread: Fine Translucent
Tail: Orange Neer Hair
Underbody: Gold Mylar tinsel
Overbody: Gold Jelly Cord
Wing: Orange Neer Hair from tail
Eyes: 1/100-oz. lead eyes

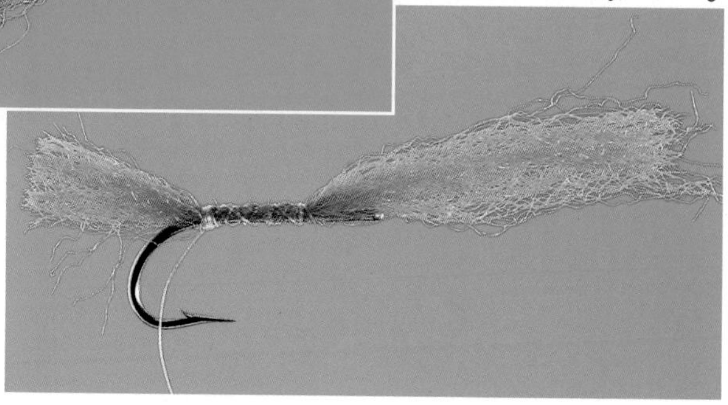

Orange Neer Hair mounted to form tail, underbody, and wing.

Andy's Spearing

Comments: After finishing this fly, the eyes, head, and shellback are coated with Loon Hard Head.

Overall length: 3″ on #1/0
Pattern type: Spearing
Primarily designed for: Striped bass, bluefish
Submitted by: The Fly Fishing Shop (Far Hills, New Jersey)
Originated by: Andy Sutton
Tied by: Andy Sutton

Hook: Mustad 34007, #1/0
Thread: Fine Translucent thread
Tail: Polar bear Super Hair or Ultra Hair flanked with silver Krystal Flash
Underbody: Pearlescent Mylar tinsel
Overbody: Silver flake Jelly Cord
Shellback: Seafoam green (or chartreuse) Super Hair or Ultra Hair, extending to tip of tail
Eyes: 3/16″ silver prism Stick-on eyes

Artistic Flies Spearing

Overall length: 3″ on #2 hook
Pattern type: Spearing
Primarily designed for: Striped bass
Also effective on: Bluefish, weakfish, false albacore, bonito
Submitted by: The Camp-Site (Huntington Station, New York)
Originated by: Amedeo J. Forzano
Tied by: Amedeo J. Forzano

Hook: Daiichi X Point, #2
Thread: Clear monofilament
Tail: White Craft Fur
Wing: Olive Craft Fur over white Craft Fur, flanked by silver Krystal Flash
Belly: White Craft Fur
Throat: Red Craft Fur
Eyes: Witchcraft Stick-on eyes, silver with black pupils
Head: Epoxy over head and eyes

Big Eye Clouser
(Blue/White)

Top view

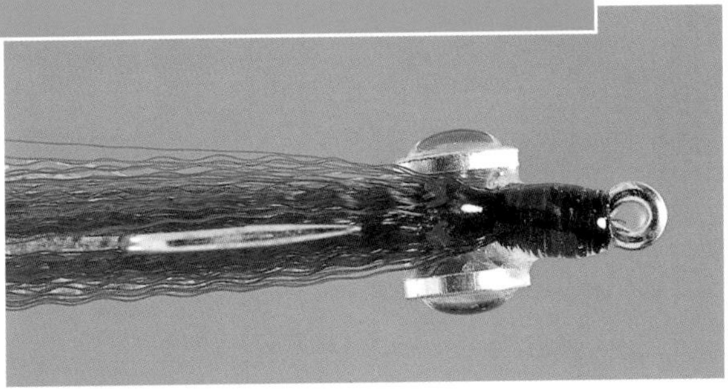

Overall length: 5″ on #2/0 hook
Pattern type: Baitfish
Primarily designed for: Striped bass
Also effective on: Black drum, redfish, bluefish, false albacore, tuna
Submitted by: Angler's Lab Outfitters (Virginia Beach, Virginia)
Originated by: Pete Bregant version of Bob Clouser design
Tied by: Steve Burton

Hook: Mustad 7766, #2/0
Thread: White Flat waxed nylon
Wing: Blue Super Hair over smoke Krystal Flash over white Super Hair
Belly: White Super Hair over blue Krystal Flash
Gills: Band of red thread
Eyes: Medium Spirit River Deep See Aluminum Eyes with silver 3-D Molded Stick-on eyes inserts
Head: White tying thread colored blue on top with permanent marker to match wing color; coated with epoxy

Big Eye Clouser
(Seafoam/Chartreuse)

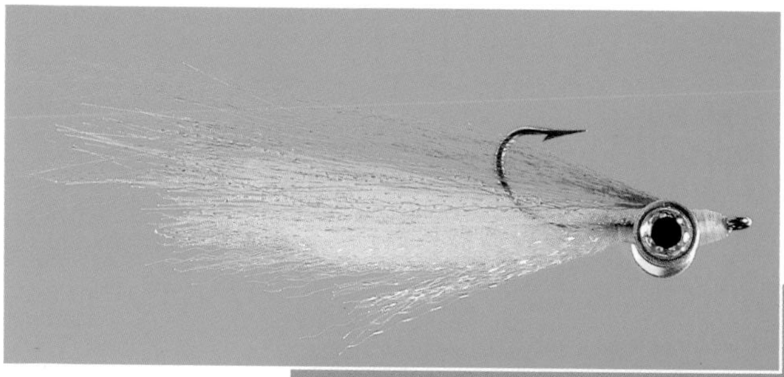

Top view

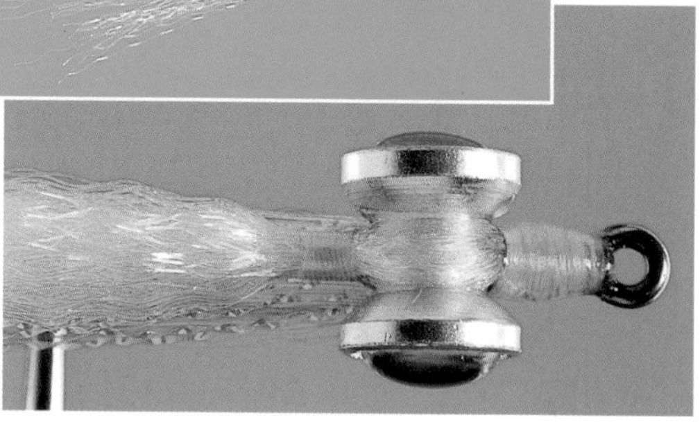

Overall length: 4 1/4" on #1/0 hook
Pattern type: Baitfish
Primarily designed for: Striped bass
Also effective on: Redfish, black drum, bluefish, false albacore, sea trout
Submitted by: Angler's Lab Outfitters (Virginia Beach, Virginia)
Originated by: Steve Burton version of Bob Clouser design
Tied by: Steve Burton

Hook: Mustad 34007, #1/0
Thread: Chartreuse Flat waxed nylon
Wing: Seafoam Super Hair over chartreuse Super Hair over pearl Krystal Flash
Belly: White Super Hair
Eyes: Medium Spirit River Deep See Aluminum eyes with prizma silver 3-D Molded Stick-on eyes inserts

Big Mac Clouser

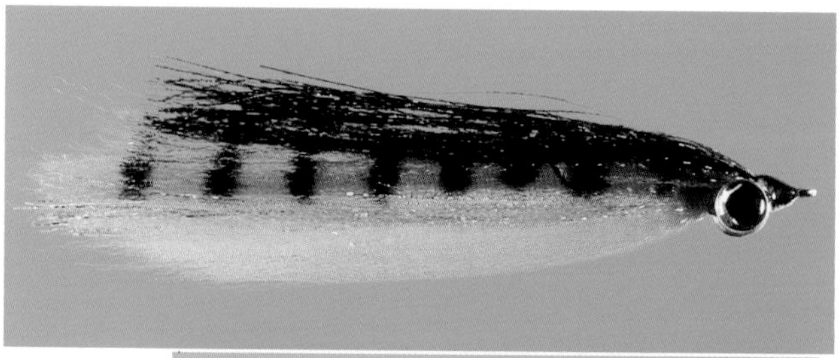

Top view

Overall length: 6 3/4" on #3/0 hook
Pattern type: Mackerel, baitfish
Primarily designed for: Striped bass
Also effective on: Tuna, false albacore, redfish, black drum
Submitted by: Angler's Lab Outfitters (Virginia Beach, Virginia)
Originated by: Pete Bregant version of Bob Clouser design
Tied by: Pete Bregant

Hook: Mustad 34011, #3/0
Thread: White Flat waxed nylon
Wing: Black holographic tinsel over green Super Hair over olive Super Hair over pearl Krystal Flash; vertical bars added with permanent black marker
Belly: White Super Hair over silver holographic tinsel
Eyes: Large gold Spirit River Deep See Aluminum Eyes with 3-D Molded Stick-on eyes inserts
Head: White thread colored green on top with permanent marker to match wing color; coated with epoxy

Black Death Clouser

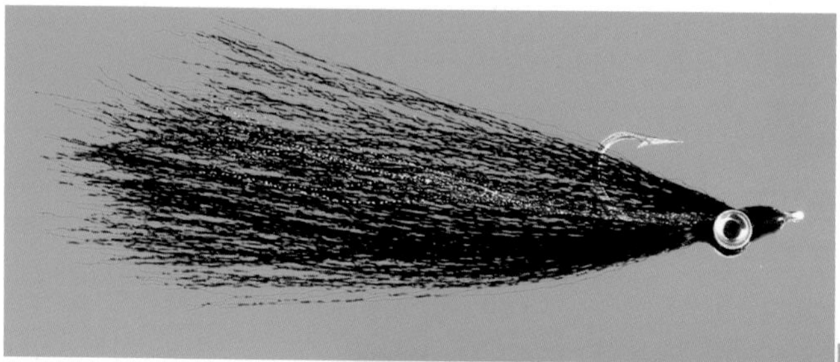

Bottom view

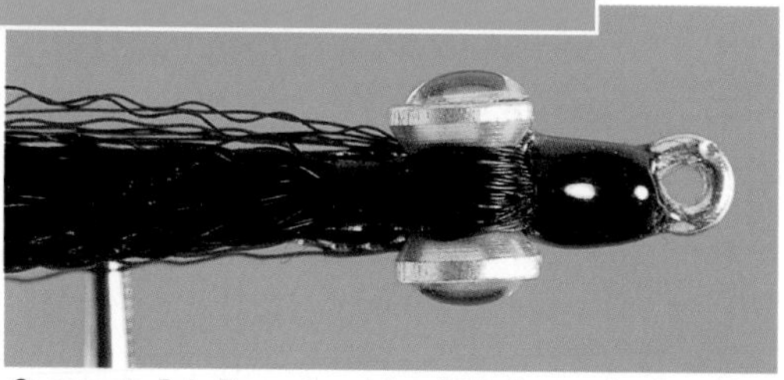

Overall length: 5" on #2/0 hook
Pattern type: Eel
Primarily designed for: Striped bass
Also effective on: Redfish
Submitted by: Angler's Lab Outfitters (Virginia Beach, Virginia)
Originated by: Pete Bregant version of Bob Clouser design
Tied by: Pete Bregant

Hook: Mustad 34007, #4/0-#1
Thread: Black Flat waxed nylon
Wing: Black Super Hair over silver Krystal Flash
Belly: Black Super Hair
Eyes: Small Spirit River Deep See Aluminum Barbell Eyes with silver 3-D Molded Stick-on eyes inserts; head and eyes coated with epoxy

Comments: Pete Bregant explains, "This fly was developed for night fishing stripers at the Chesapeake Bay Bridge Tunnel; it's fished in the shadow/light line." Using gold Krystal Flash and gold eyes makes a good redfish pattern.

Bluefish Fly

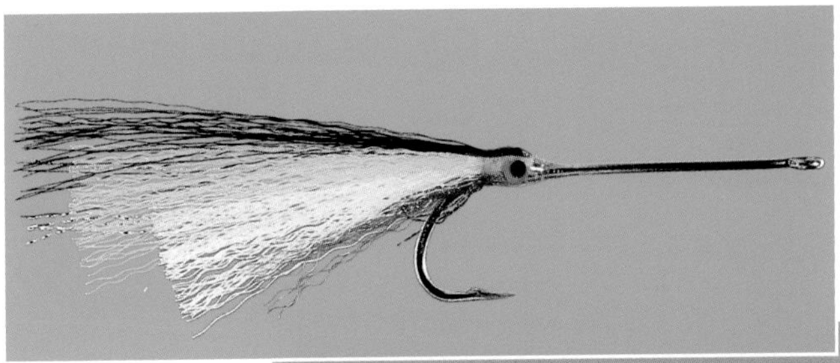

Top view

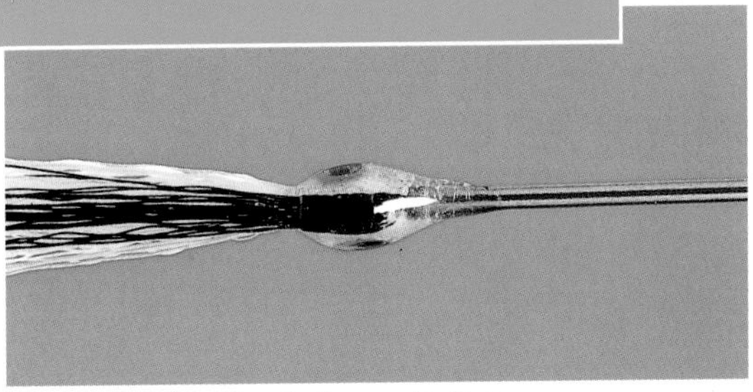

Comments: This pattern is also good in blue.

Overall length: 4" on #2/0 hook
Pattern type: Baitfish
Primarily designed for: Bluefish
Also effective on: Striped bass
Submitted by: The Camp-Site (Huntington Station, New York)
Originated by: Unknown
Tied by: Amedeo J. Forzano

Hook: TMC 911 or Mustad 92608, #2/0
Thread: Clear monofilament
Wing: Black Ultra Hair over fluorescent green Ultra Hair over silver Krystal Flash over white Ultra Hair over red Ultra Hair
Throat: Red Krystal Flash
Eyes: Witchcraft Stick-on eyes, orange with black pupils; head and eyes coated with epoxy

Bozo Bunker

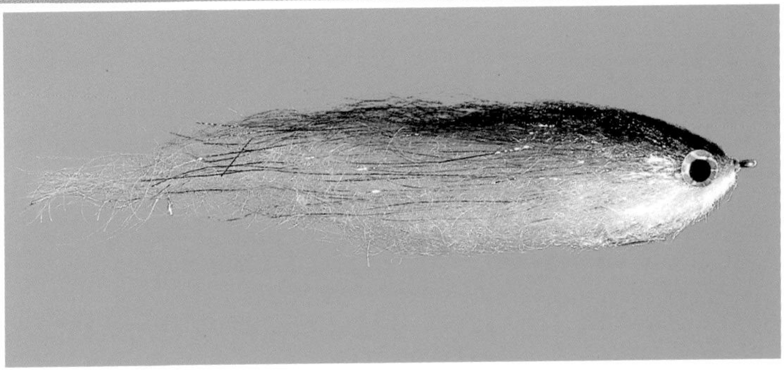

Overall length: 9 1/2" on #6/0 hook
Pattern type: Menhaden or herring
Primarily designed for: Striped bass
Also effective on: Bluefish
Submitted by: The Fly Hatch (Shrewsbury, New Jersey)
Originated by: Captain Dave Chouinard
Tied by: David Frassinelli

Hook: Eagle Claw 254SS, #6/0-#3/0
Thread: Flat Nylon
Tail: 20 strands Gold Flash over yellow Super Hair
Body: White Bozo Hair tied on top and bottom of shank followed by pearl blue Rainbow Flash that shrouds the Bozo Hair. Repeat until all but 1/4" of shank is covered. Then tie in olive Bozo Hair over back
Head: White Neer Hair and pearl Lite Brite tied in layers to surround last 1/4" of shank, trimmed to shape and colored with Pantone markers to match color of fly back
Eyes: Large Mylar

Bozo Hair Bunker

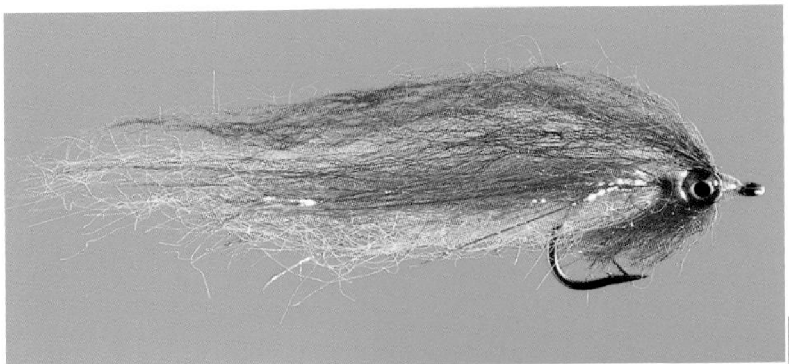

Top: blue and white version; bottom: blue and pink version.

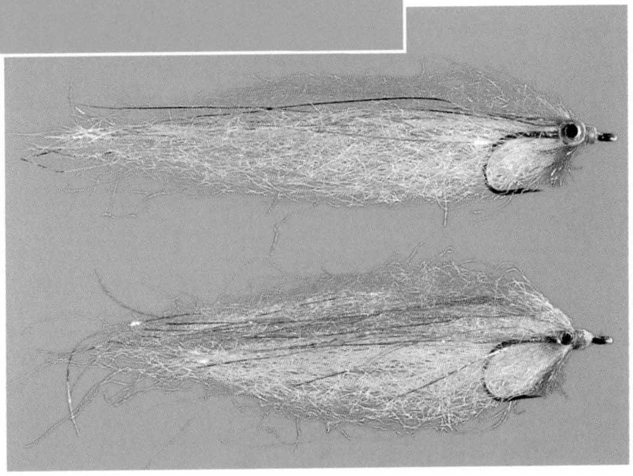

Overall length: 5 1/2" on #2/0 hook
Pattern type: Baby bunker or herring
Primarily designed for: Striped bass
Also effective on: Bluefish, false albacore, snook, cobia
Submitted by: Northrop's Landing (Westport, Connecticut)
Originated by: Captain Jeff Northrop
Tied by: Captain Jeff Northrop

Hook: TMC 800S, #2/-#1/0
Thread: Orvis Monocord
Tail: Hot pink Bozo Hair topped with pink Orvis Glimmer (#65); (pearl Glimmer only for blue/white version; pink Glimmer only for blue/pink version)
Wing: Green Bozo Hair over white Bozo hair (blue/white version: blue Bozo Hair over blue Glimmer over white Bozo Hair; blue/pink version: blue Bozo Hair over pink Glimmer over white Bozo Hair)
Belly: White Bozo Hair (blue/pink version: white Bozo Hair over pale pink Bozo Hair)
Gills: Salmon pink Orvis Light Bright (#63)
Eyes: White solid plastic eyes; mount with crisscross wraps over stem, then glue

Bruce's Bay Anchovy

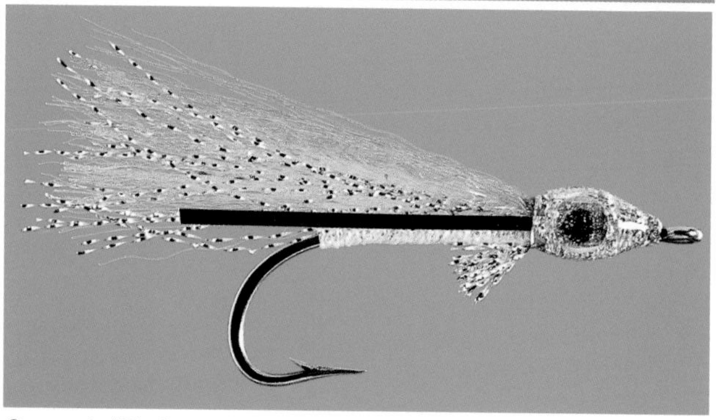

Overall length: 2" on #2 hook
Pattern type: Bay anchovy
Primarily designed for: Striped bass
Also effective on: False albacore, bluefish, Spanish mackerel, and most saltwater species
Submitted by: The Fisherman's Edge (Baltimore, Maryland)
Originated by: Joe Bruce
Tied by: Joe Bruce

Hook: Mustad 34011, #2
Thread: Fine clear monofilament
Body: Kreinik 1/8" pearl flat ribbon (or wide holographic tinsel or Mylar tubing)
Throat: 15-20 strands silver Krystal Flash
Wing: 12-15 strands dark gray Ultra Hair over 12-15 strands smoke Ultra Hair over 12-15 strands silver Krystal Flash over 12-15 strands polar bear Ultra Hair
Lateral line: Wide silver tinsel
Head: Silver Krystal Flash, wrapped
Eyes: 3mm Stick-on eyes; head and eyes coated with small amount of epoxy

Comments: "The bay anchovy," explains Joe Bruce, "is a significant food source for blues, Spanish mackerel, stripers, and false albacore during the summer and fall, and is one of the food sources most commonly associated with breaking fish during these times. This one of the flies that 'match the hatch' in the salt."

Bruce's Bunker

Overall length: 5" on #3/0 hook
Pattern type: Baby bunker
Primarily designed for: Striped bass, bluefish
Submitted by: North Country Outfitters (Lafayette, New Jersey)
Originated by: Bruce Fradl
Tied by: Bruce Fradl

Hook: Mustad 34011, #3/0
Thread: Clear mono .006"
Tail: White bucktail
Body: Opalescent white Estaz #1
Belly: White bucktail
Throat: Red calf tail
Wing: Peacock herl over white bucktail
Eyes: Witchcraft gold #3 1/2
Head: Devcon 5-minute epoxy

Bruce's Crab Colored Clouser Deep Minnow (BCCCDM)

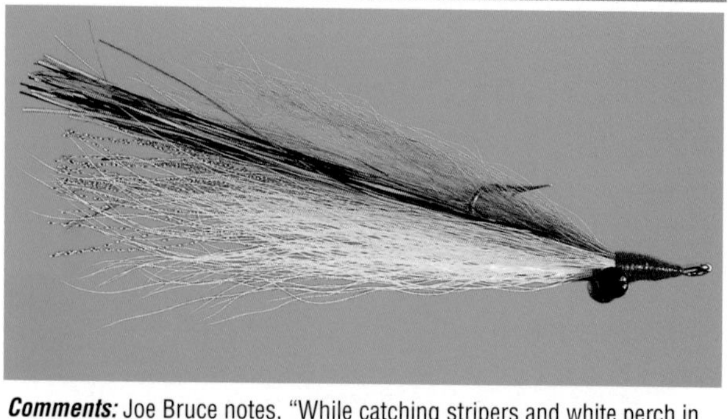

Overall length: 4 1/4" on #2/0 hook
Pattern type: Crab, baitfish
Primarily designed for: Striped bass
Also effective on: Just about everything
Submitted by: The Fisherman's Edge (Baltimore, Maryland)
Originated by: Joe Bruce version of Clouser Deep Minnow
Tied by: Joe Bruce

Hook: Mustad 34007, #2/0-#4
Thread: Fire orange Flat waxed nylon
Eyes: 1/36-oz. lead barbell, ends colored with permanent black marker
Wing: 20-30 fibers olive bucktail over 25-30 strands copper Flashabou over 20-30 fibers tan bucktail over 20-25 strands gold Krystal Flash over 20-30 fibers white bucktail

Comments: Joe Bruce notes, "While catching stripers and white perch in the tributaries and having them spit up small rock crabs and blue crabs, I started thinking about a way to imitate these small creatures without the tying time needed for normal crab patterns. I needed some weight and the right combinations of colors to accomplish this. The Clouser was the logical choice. Natural coloration takes the guesswork away from the fish, and the colors in this fly are all natural to saltwater. The BCCCDM has accounted for some larger fish when fished next to the same size Clouser in more standard colors. I like to fish this fly with a definite pause in between strips; the strikes will come as the fly drops, and they are usually hard, which reinforces the theory that fish are taking the fly as a crab. Fish generally hit crabs and crustaceans with enough force to kill the bait so they won't be bitten." When tying small sizes of this pattern, reduce the wing bulk; on a #4 hook, for instance, about 15 strands of each wing material are sufficient.

Bruce's Crab Colored Half & Half

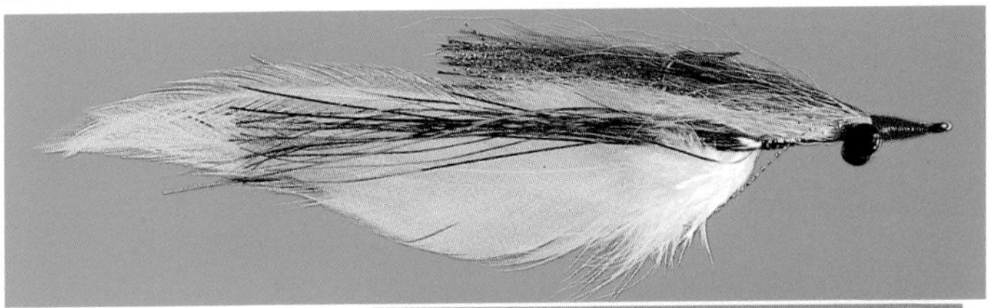

Overall length: 6 1/4" on #4/0 hook
Pattern type: Crab, baitfish
Primarily designed for: Striped bass
Also effective on: Other predatory fish
Submitted by: The Fisherman's Edge (Baltimore, Maryland)
Originated by: Joe Bruce adaptation of Clouser Minnow and Lefty's Deceiver
Tied by: Joe Bruce

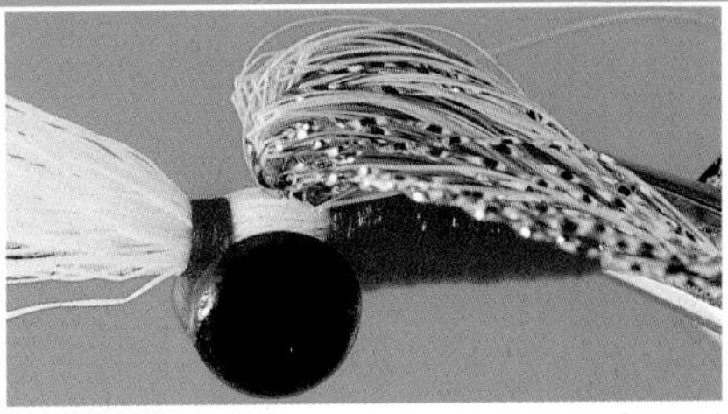

Detail showing head construction.

Hook: Mustad #34011, #4/0
Thread: Fire orange Flat waxed nylon
Eye: 1/16-oz. lead barbell, ends colored with black permanent marker
Tail: Four white saddle hackles, 4 1/2" to 6" long, flanked by copper Flashabou
Body: Wide gold tinsel or saltwater Flashabou
Wing: 25-30 fibers olive bucktail over 25-30 strands copper Flashabou over 25-30 fibers tan bucktail over 25 strands gold Krystal Flash over 25-30 fibers white bucktail

Comments: Tyer Joe Bruce explains, "This is my variation of the Crab Colored Clouser using two of the most popular saltwater flies in the world—the Clouser Deep Minnow and Lefty's Deceiver. This is not a new fly or particular pattern, but a tying style that was a natural step from the success of the two original flies. The Half & Half adds greater length and bulk than can be achieved using bucktail, which has limited length, while the saddle hackles offer the undulating image of the Deceiver." Note that the white bucktail is mounted ahead of the eyes, then bound down behind the eyes with a band of thread. The remaining wing materials are all mounted and bound down ahead of the eyes.

Bruce's Crystal Crab

Overall length: 3 1/4" on #1/0 hook
Pattern type: Crab
Primarily designed for: Striped bass, redfish
Submitted by: The Fisherman's Edge (Baltimore, Maryland)
Originated by: Joe Bruce
Tied by: Joe Bruce

Hook: Mustad 34007, #1/0 and #4
Thread: Fire orange Flat waxed nylon
Claws: Natural deer body hair
Eyes: Two 4-bead lengths of large bead chain, painted black (for #4 hook, use small plastic eyes)
Body: One strand each of olive and tan Flash Chenille, 12" long, standard size (use micro Flash Chenille for #4 hook), twisted together and wrapped
Legs: Green or natural round rubber, mottled with black marker, or Sili-Legs

Comments: Joe Bruce notes that while the pattern described here uses bead-chain eyes to get the fly to the bottom, it can also be tied with plastic bead eyes and fished on the surface around structure—a good approach at night around lighted docks and piers.

Bottom view

Bruce's Crystal Shrimp

Top: size 1/0 fly using standard Flash Chenille; Bottom: Top view of fly in main photo.

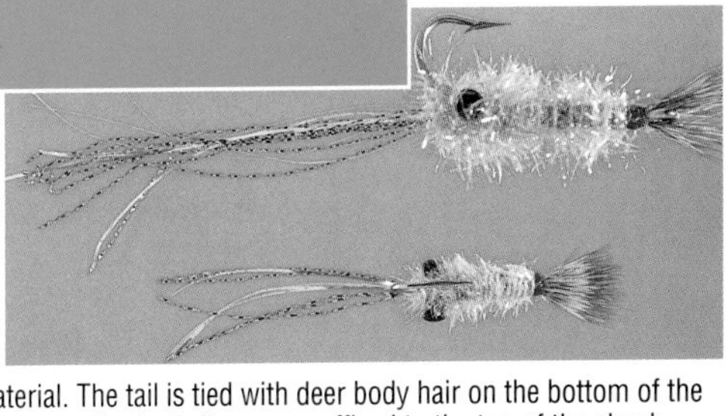

Overall length: 2 1/2" on #4 hook (3 3/4" on #1/0 hook)
Pattern type: Shrimp
Primarily designed for: Striped bass
Also effective on: Perch, redfish, speckled sea trout, bonefish, and other flats species
Submitted by: The Fisherman's Edge (Baltimore, Maryland)
Originated by: Joe Bruce
Tied by: Joe Bruce

Hook: Mustad 34007, #1/0 and #4
Thread: Fire orange Flat waxed nylon
Eyes: 1/50-oz. lead barbell (1/36-oz. for #1/0 hook), ends colored black with permanent marker
Antennae: 4 strands pearl Flashabou mixed with 4 strands copper Krystal Flash (6 strands each for #1/0 hook)
Body: Tan micro Flash Chenille or Estaz (standard size for #1/0 hook)
Tail: Natural deer body hair

Comments: Joe Bruce notes, "This is a fast, easy, and durable fly pattern that represents the saltwater shrimp found around pilings and underwater structure. One of the least recognized aspects of this fly is the positioning of the tail material. The tail is tied with deer body hair on the bottom of the hook, which rides point-up because the barbell eyes are affixed to the top of the shank. The position of the deer hair accomplishes two purposes. First, it looks like the tail of a shrimp when seen from above; second, and most importantly, when the deer hair softens up in the water, it tends to flare out. This causes the fly to dart from side to side when retrieved with short strips of line, imitating the darting motion of a real shrimp. The fly can be tied in other colors. The three best are tan, pearl, and white (especially for bonefish), but root beer and pink chenille have proven very successful on redfish and sea trout."

Bruce's Eel Fly

Overall length: 8 1/4" on #2/0 hooks
Pattern type: Eel
Primarily designed for: Striped bass
Also effective on: Bluefish, cobia
Submitted by: The Fisherman's Edge (Baltimore, Maryland)
Originated by: Joe Bruce
Tied by: Joe Bruce

Hook: Mustad 34007, #5/0-#1/0; 2 hooks joined with 30-lb. Dacron as explained below
Thread: Fire orange Flat waxed nylon
Body: Rusty brown rabbit strip (or black, olive, purple or chartreuse)
Tail on front hook: 15-20 strands each of copper Flashabou and gold Krystal Flash
Body on front hook: Rabbit strip, palmered
Throat: 15-20 strands red Krystal Flash
Head: Tying thread
Eyes: 3mm Stick-on eyes, silver with black pupils; head and eyes coated with 5-minute epoxy

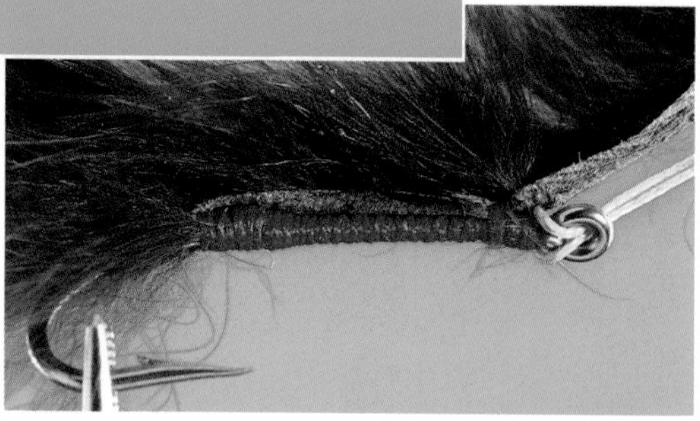

Detail of rear hook.

Comments: The rear hooks is dressed first. About 2 1/2" to 3" from the end of the rabbit strip, push the hook point through the skin side of the strip; then about 1/8" from this hole, push the point back through the strip, from the fur side to the skin side. Put the hook in a vise and cover the shank with thread. Bind down the rabbit fur between the 2 holes pierced in the hide, separating the fur carefully to cinch down the hide. Pull the fur strip rearward, advance the thread to the eye. Pull the strip forward and bind down behind the hook eye. Whip-finish around shank behind eye and clip.

Cut a piece of Dacron backing or Spider Wire fishing line about 10" long. Double over, and put both ends through eye of rear hook. Put front hook in vise. Lash down tag ends of Dacron to top of shank; put tag ends through hook eye, and bind tags to underside of shank, all the way to the bend. Tie in tinsel tail.

Bring rabbit strip from rear hook over top of shank. Do not pull tight. There should be a little slack. Bind down strip at bend of hook. Palmer strip forward and tie off behind hook eye. Dress throat, head, and eyes.

Bruce's Epoxy Spoon Fly

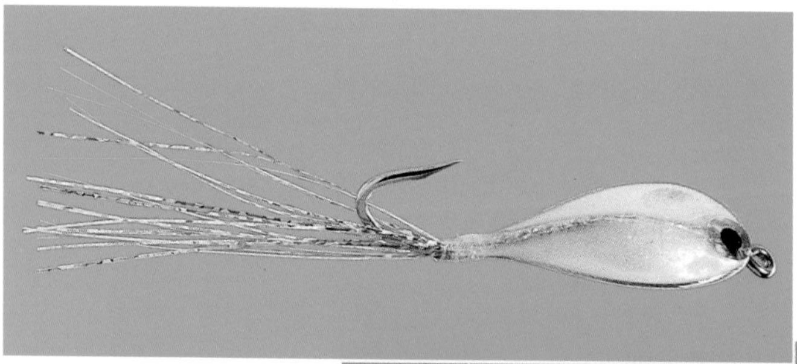

Top: side view
Bottom: Bottom view of chartreuse version.

Overall length: 3 1/4" on #2/0 hook
Pattern type: Bay anchovy, silverside
Primarily designed for: Striped bass, bluefish
Also effective on: Spanish mackerel, and virtually any predatory species
Submitted by: The Fisherman's Edge (Baltimore, Maryland)
Originated by: Joe Bruce
Tied by: Joe Bruce

Hook: Mustad #34011, #2/0, #2, and #6; bent to shape
Thread: Clear fine monofilament
Tail: Holographic tinsel (or Flashabou of choice)
Body frame: Surflon nylon-coated wire; 15-lb. for #2 and #6, 20-lb. for #2/0
Body: Devcon 5-minute epoxy, colored with pearl pigment (chartreuse for chartreuse version), with green and soft blue Glick ultrafine glitter
Eyes: Stick-on eyes, silver with black pupils; 3mm eyes for #2 and #6, 4mm eyes for #2/0

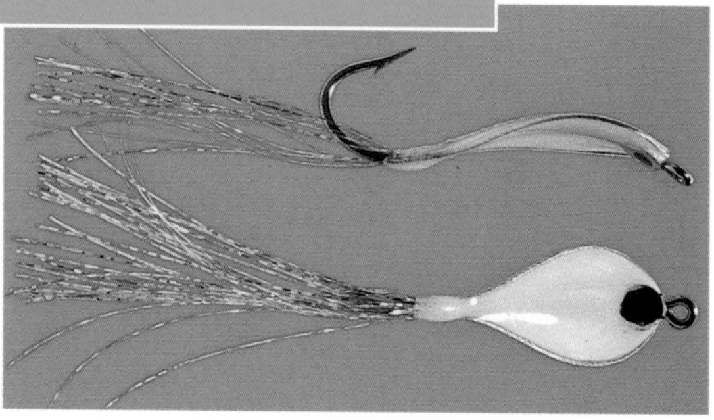

Comments: Joe Bruce explains, "This is a fly lure created specifically to take fish that are breaking at the surface. It has the added bonus of handling bluefish and Spanish mackerel. I hated to have to change my fly each time that bluefish would show up during a surface feeding frenzy. The epoxy body holds up well to these toothy critters. It has also proved effective in searching underwater."

To bend the hook to shape, use a needle-nose pliers. Grasp the shank behind the eye, with the hook point facing you, and start bending the shank in a direction opposite the hook point. Work for a smooth, slight bend along the first 1/3 of the shank.

Tie the tail materials atop and underneath the shank. Then attach the middle of a 4" length of Surflon wire crosswise behind the hook eye, using crisscross wraps. Loop one end of the wire to the rear of the hook, forming a "bow" around one side of the shank, and tie off the wire. Repeat with the other side to make a second "bow," completing a spoon-shaped frame of the desired size. Clip and bind down the wire tags. Attach the eyes to the hook shank, atop and underneath, inside the wire frame.

Using a straightened paper clip, mix epoxy and whatever pigment and glitter you desire. Apply the epoxy first around the eyes, then to both sides of the wire tie-off point at the hook bend. Pick up a large dollop of epoxy and lay it around the eyes and try to pull the mixture back to the hook bend. Work on one side of the frame at a time until both sides are filled in, making a "skin" of epoxy inside the frame. Remove any excess epoxy around the center of the shank—the tied-down tail tinsel should show through—and around the eyes. Rotate the spoon on a motor dryer or vise for 5-minutes or until epoxy sets.

Bruce's Herring

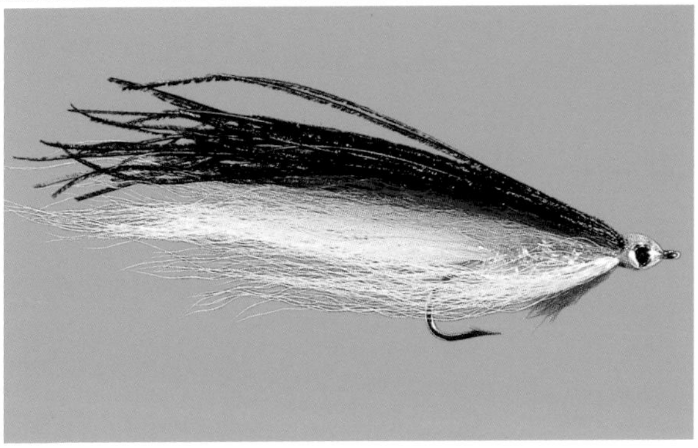

Overall length: 5¾" on #4/0 hook
Pattern type: Herring
Primarily designed for: Striped bass, bluefish
Also effective on: On #1/0 hook (fly 25%-30% smaller) for weakfish
Submitted by: North Country Outfitters (Lafayette, New Jersey)
Originated by: Bruce Fradl
Tied by: Bruce Fradl

Hook: Mustad 34011, #4/0
Thread: Clear mono .006"
Tail: White bucktail
Body: Pink Estaz #36
Belly: White bucktail
Throat: Red calf tail
Wing: Peacock herl over blue bucktail over pink bucktail over white bucktail
Eyes: Witchcraft #3 1/2 gold
Head: Devcon 5-minute epoxy

Bruce's Sea-Ductive (Blue)

Overall length: 5 1/2" on #3/0 hook
Pattern type: Attractor
Primarily designed for: Striped bass, bluefish
Submitted by: North Country Outfitters (Lafayette, New Jersey)
Originated by: Bruce Fradl
Tied by: Bruce Fradl

Hook: Mustad 34011, #3/0
Thread: Clear mono .006"
Tail: Blue bucktail over 6 strands blue holographic tinsel over white bucktail
Body: Danville Depth Ray fluorescent blue nylon, coated with Devcon 5-minute epoxy
Eyes: Witchcraft #3 silver

Bruce's Sea-Ductive (Chartreuse)

Overall length: 5 1/2" on #3/0 hook
Pattern type: Attractor
Primarily designed for: Striped bass, bluefish
Also effective on: On #2 hook for false albacore and weakfish
Submitted by: North Country Outfitters (Lafayette, New Jersey)
Originated by: Bruce Fradl
Tied by: Bruce Fradl

Hook: Mustad 34011, #3/0
Thread: Clear mono .006"
Tail: Chartreuse bucktail over 6 strands pearl Krystal Flash over white bucktail
Body: Chartreuse UNI-Stretch, coated with Devcon 5-minute epoxy
Eyes: Witchcraft #3 silver

Bruce's Sea-Ductive (White)

Overall length: 5 1/2" on 3/0 hook
Pattern type: General attractor
Primarily designed for: Striped bass, bluefish
Also effective on: On #2 hook for false albacore and weakfish
Submitted by: North Country Outfitters (Lafayette, New Jersey)
Originated by: Bruce Fradl
Tied by: Bruce Fradl

Hook: Mustad 34011, #3/0
Thread: Clear mono .006"
Tail: White bucktail mixed with 6 strands pearl Flashabou
Body: White UNI-Stretch, coated with Devcon 5-minute epoxy
Eyes: Witchcraft #3 green

Bruce's Ultra Hair Silversides

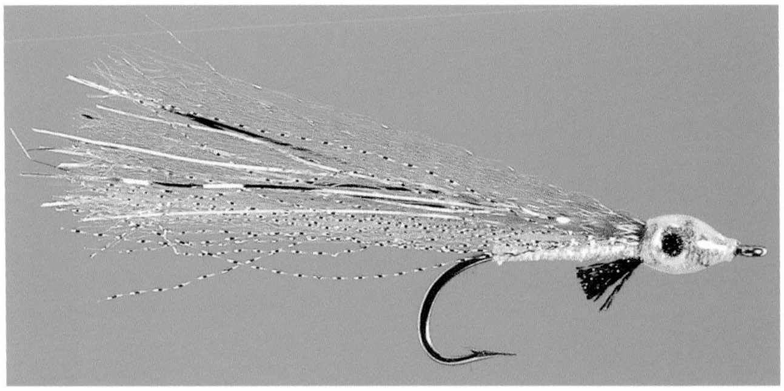

Overall length: 3" on #2 hook
Pattern type: Silverside minnow
Primarily designed for: Striped bass, false albacore
Also effective on: Most predatory species
Submitted by: The Fisherman's Edge (Baltimore, Maryland)
Originated by: Joe Bruce
Tied by: Joe Bruce

Hook: Mustad 34011, #2
Thread: Fine clear monofilament
Body: Kreinik 1/8" pearl ribbon
Throat: Red Krystal Flash
Wing: 10-15 strands olive Ultra Hair over 10-15 strands blue Ultra Hair over 12-15 strands silver Krystal Flash mixed with 12-15 strands silver Flashabou over 10-15 strands neon pink Ultra Hair over 10-15 strands polar bear Ultra Hair
Head: Pearl Krystal Flash
Eyes: 3mm Stick-on eyes, silver with black pupils; head and eyes coated with 5-minute epoxy

Comments: Unlike many silverside patterns, this one relies on translucent, rather than opaque materials. This pattern uses four colors of nylon Ultra Hair to create the shading of the natural baitfish, reproducing the subtle color changes from top to bottom.

Bushwick Special

Bottom view

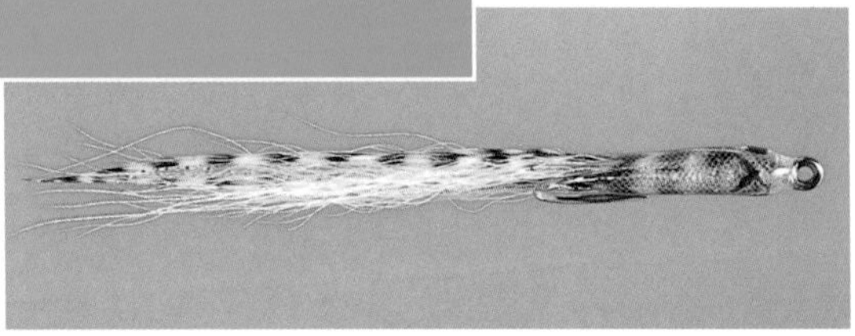

Overall length: 3 1/2" on #1 hook
Pattern type: Anchovy
Primarily designed for: False albacore, bluefish, striped bass
Submitted by: Urban Angler Ltd. (New York, New York)
Originated by: Edwin Valentin
Tied by: Edwin Valentin

Hook: Mustad 34007, #1/0-#2
Thread: Fine monofilament
Tail: Tan bucktail over root beer Krystal Flash over white bucktail; flanked by 1 grade 3 grizzly on each side, all attached behind hook eye
Body: Flat pearl Diamond Braid wrapped around shank; tailing materials drawn to top half shank and pulled back; entire body coated with Corsair 5-minute epoxy.
Gills: Drawn with red waterproof marker
Eyes: 2mm Stick-on eyes

Chesapeake Gurgle Bug

Overall length: 4 1/4" on 2/0 hook
Pattern type: Attractor
Primarily designed for: Striped bass
Also effective on: Snook, sea trout
Submitted by: Chesapeake Fly & Bait Company (Arnold, Maryland)
Originated by: Jack Gartside
Tied by: Jim Hester

Hook: Mustad 34007 or other equivalent saltwater hook, #4/0-#2
Thread: Fluorescent orange Danville 3/0 Monocord or Flat Waxed Nylon
Tail: 4 pairs yellow neck or saddle hackle flanked with 6 strands holographic Mylar per side
Body: Pearl Cactus Chenille
Hackle: Red neck or saddle
Shellback: Red 3mm closed-cell foam
Legs (optional): Rubber legs
Eyes (optional): Doll eyes, glued
Weed guard (optional): 30-lb. hard Mason nylon

Bottom view

Comments: Tyer Jim Hester explains, "This fly is an adaptation of Jack Gartside's 'Gurgler.' It can be tied in any color combinations. The pattern floats in, not on, the surface film and is very light and easy to cast." The fly is particularly effective on Chesapeake Bay tidal rivers and the Susquehanna flats.

Chesapeake Sparkle Blue Crab

Top view

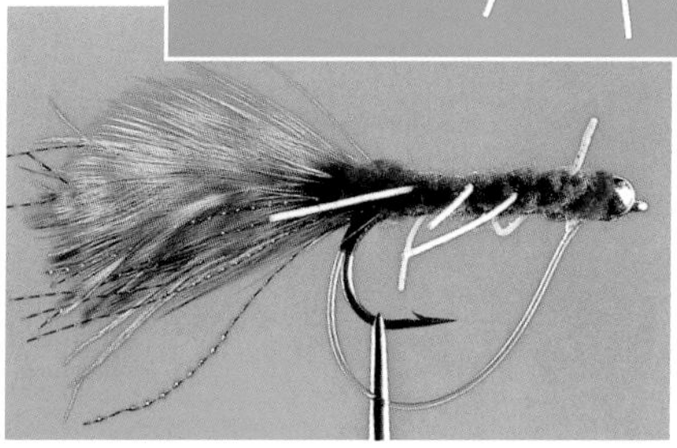

Overall length: 3 1/2" on #2/0 hook
Pattern type: Blue crab
Primarily designed for: Striped bass
Also effective on: Permit, croaker, redfish, bonefish
Submitted by: Chesapeake Fly & Bait Company (Arnold, Maryland)
Originated by: Jim Hester
Tied by: Jim Hester

Hook: Mustad 34007, #2/0-#4
Thread: Olive or dark blue Danville 3/0 Monocord
Weed guard: 30-lb. hard Mason nylon
Claws: Olive ostrich herl flanked with copper Krystal Flash flanked by 3 pairs cree hackle feathers
Body: Olive and blue acrylic rug yarn; belly and back coated with Crystal Iris fabric paint
Legs: White or blue round rubber or Sili-Legs
Eyes: 1/24-oz. plated barbell eyes

Comments: "This fly," notes Jim Hester, "can be fished in open, shallow waters but is best suited for use around pilings, rock piles, and along sod banks. Stripers check out these areas on a falling tide looking for crabs, especially soft crabs."

Chesapeake Special

Overall length: 4 3/4" on #2/0 hook
Pattern type: Bay anchovy
Primarily designed for: Striped bass
Also effective on: Bluefish, flounder, Spanish mackerel, bonito
Submitted by: Chesapeake Fly & Bait Company (Arnold, Maryland)
Originated by: Jim Hester
Tied by: Jim Hester

Hook: Mustad 32608N, #4/0-#2/0
Thread: Fire orange Danville Flat waxed nylon
Tail: Pearl Mylar from body, unraveled
Body: Large pearl Mylar tubing, wrapped
Wing: 10-20 strands peacock herl over blue bucktail over fluorescent blue bucktail over white bucktail that encircles hook shank
Lateral line: 10-15 strands silver holographic Mylar
Head: Tying thread coated with epoxy with fine pearl glitter mixed in
Eyes: Painted, white with black pupils

Chesapeake Striper Special

Overall length: 4 1/2" on #2/0 hook
Pattern type: Attractor
Primarily designed for: Striped bass
Submitted by: Chesapeake Fly & Bait Company (Arnold, Maryland)
Originated by: Jim Hester
Tied by: Jim Hester

Hook: Mustad 34007, #3/0-#2/0
Thread: Red Danville 3/0 Monocord
Tail: Yellow bucktail over white bucktail, equal amounts
Body: Pearl Micro Cactus Chenille or Crystal Chenille
Wing: Green bucktail over chartreuse bucktail over white bucktail, equal amounts; flanked with 6-10 strands holographic Mylar per side
Eyes: Painted, white with black pupils

Comments: "This fly," notes Jim Hester, "is tied in the Joe Brooks Blonde style. The tail is 1 1/2 to 2 times longer than the hook, and the wing extends to the tip of the tail. It is an extremely effective fly in the Susquehanna and Potomac Rivers for stripers."

Clarabelle Clouser

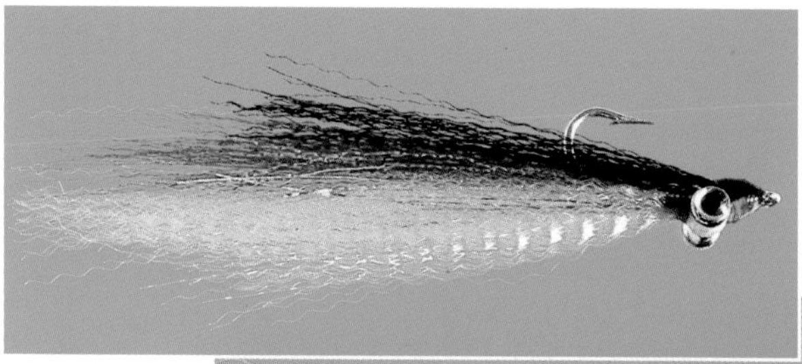

Top view

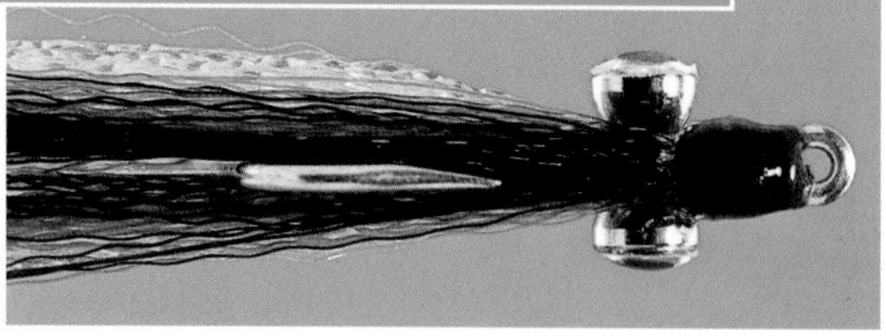

Comments: Ron Russell notes, "The name 'Clarabelle' is a result of a friend who was catching fish on a Bozo pattern. To be in line with his nomenclature, I called this fly a 'Clarabelle' after the clown on the old Howdy Doody Show."

Overall length: 4" on #2/0 hook
Pattern type: Menhaden, bay herring
Primarily designed for: Speckled sea trout
Also effective on: Redfish, striped bass, bluefish, cobia, weakfish, flounder, false albacore
Submitted by: Angler's Lab Outfitters (Virginia Beach, Virginia)
Originated by: Ron Russell version of Bob Clouser design
Tied by: Ron Russell

Hook: Mustad 7766, #2/0-#4
Thread: White Flat waxed nylon
Wing: Black Super Hair over Kelly green Super Hair over pearl Krystal Flash
Belly: White (or pale olive) Super Hair
Gills: Band of red Flat waxed nylon
Eyes: 1/4" Spirit River Deep See Aluminum Eyes with silver 3-D Molded Stick-on eyes inserts
Head: White tying thread colored black on top and green underneath with Prisma Pen markers, band of red tying thread for nose; coated with 5-minute epoxy

Clouser Minnow

Bottom view

Comments: Ron Russell explains, "This pattern works very well on the lower Chesapeake Bay and coastal North Carolina. Fish it on a short 4'-5' leader and a fast-sinking line to get the fly on or near the bottom, and use a slow, steady retrieve. I use sparse amounts of Krystal Flash and add the red throat to simulate flared gills and an open mouth."

Overall length: 2 1/2" on #4 hook
Pattern type: Menhaden, herring, of lower Chesapeake Bay
Primarily designed for: Speckled sea trout
Also effective on: Redfish, striped bass, bluefish, flounder
Submitted by: Angler's Lab Outfitters (Virginia Beach, Virginia)
Originated by: Bob Clouser
Tied by: Ron Russell

Hook: Mustad 7766, #1/0-#4
Thread: Red Danville Flat waxed nylon
Wing: Olive bucktail over pearl Krystal Flash
Belly: Red bucktail over white bucktail
Eyes: 5/32" nickel-plated barbell eyes

C.S.'s Epoxy Spearing

Comments: Chris Sacchetti notes that tying the materials at the hook bend gives this fly more action in the water and prevents bite-offs by bluefish.

Overall length: 5 3/4" on #1 hook
Pattern type: Spearing
Primarily designed for: Bluefish, striped bass
Also effective on: Weakfish
Submitted by: Delaware River Outfitters (Pennington, New Jersey)
Originated by: Chris Sacchetti version of Bob Popovic's Surf Candy
Tied by: Chris Sacchetti

Hook: Mustad 34011, #1
Thread: Clear mono
Belly: White bucktail tied in at bend on underside of shank
Wing: Olive bucktail over chartreuse bucktail over 8-10 strands silver Flashabou over clump of pearl Flashabou clipped to ⅓ length of bucktail
Eyes: 2.5mm yellow Prism Eyes
Head: 5-minute epoxy extending just past hook bend
Gills: Red waterproof marker

C.S.'s Hardhead Mullet

Top view

Overall length: 5 1/2" on 4/0 hook
Pattern type: Finger mullet
Primarily designed for: Striped bass
Also effective on: Bluefish, weakfish
Submitted by: Delaware River Outfitters (Pennington, New Jersey)
Originated by: Chris Sacchetti
Tied by: Chris Sacchetti's version of Lou Taboury's Slab Side

Hook: Mustad 34007, #4/0
Thread: White 3/0
Tail: Large clump of white bucktail flanked with pearl Flashabou (bind butts with thread to cover)
Wing: 2 grizzly saddle feathers over 2 light gray saddle feathers over clump of white bucktail
Gills: Red Krystal Flash
Collar: Deer hair tips from spun head
Head: White deer hair, spun and clipped to shape; top colored with fabric marker; clipped portion of head coated with Super Glue
Eyes: Painted, Jones Tones Glitter Paint (yellow) with glossy black pupil

Comments: Tyer Chris Sacchetti notes that treating the head with Super Glue makes this fly easier to cast into the wind. The pattern can be adapted to imitate a variety of baitfish by altering the color. This pattern has proven highly productive along the southern New Jersey Coast and took the striped bass that won the fly-rod division of the 1998 Atlantic City Press Fishing Contest.

C.S.'s Stealth Bunker

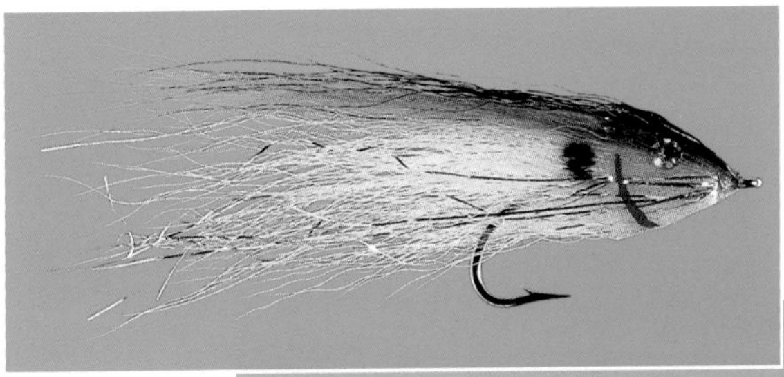

Top view

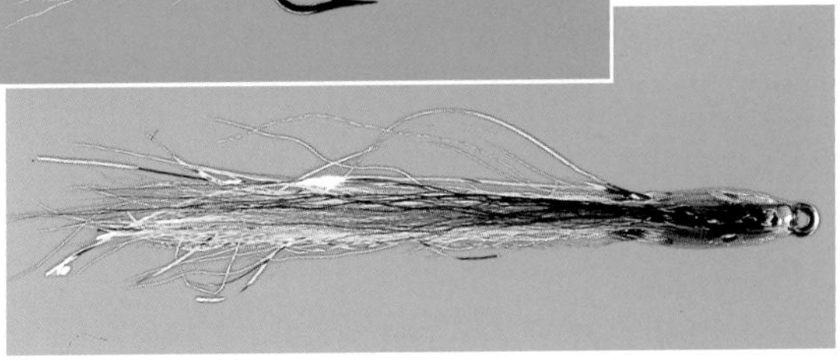

Overall length: 4 1/4" on #4/0 hook
Pattern type: Peanut bunker
Primarily designed for: Striped bass
Also effective on: Bluefish
Submitted by: Delaware River Outfitters (Pennington, New Jersey)
Originated by: Chris Sacchetti
Tied by: Chris Sacchetti

Hook: Mustad 34007, #4/0
Thread: Clear mono
Tail: White bucktail
Wing: Black bucktail over light gray bucktail over pink bucktail over white bucktail
Lateral accents: Pearl Krystal Flash and silver Flashabou
Eyes: Prismatic Stick-on eyes
Head: 5-minute epoxy from eye of hook back 1/2 shank length, formed to wedge shape
Gills: Red marker

C.S.'s Synthetic Peanut Bunker

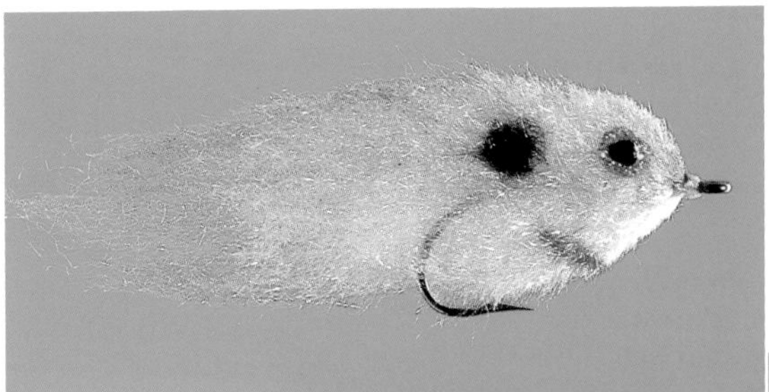

Top view

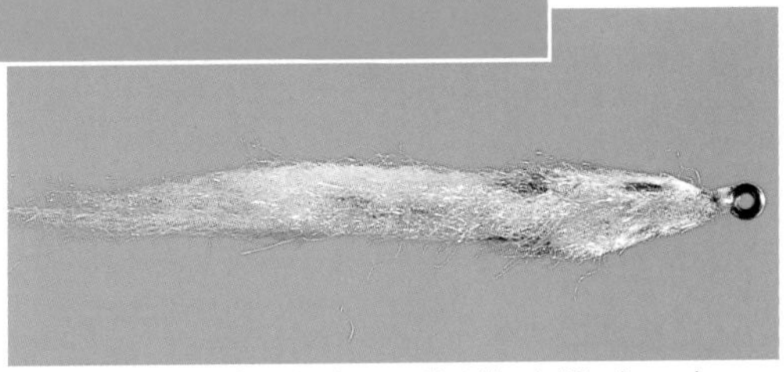

Overall length: 4 1/4" on #4/0 hook
Pattern type: Peanut bunker
Primarily designed for: Striped bass
Also effective on: Bluefish
Submitted by: Delaware River Outfitters (Pennington, New Jersey)
Originated by: Chris Sacchetti
Tied by: Chris Sacchetti

Hook: Mustad 34007, #4/0
Thread: Clear mono
Body: White Enhancer Hanks attached in small bunches along top and bottom of shank, with one small clump attached on each side of shank; brush out fibers and color with pink, light blue, light gray, and dark gray fabric markers (or colors to match local baitfish)
Eyes: Jones Tones Glitter Paint (yellow) with glossy black pupil

Comments: Chris Sacchetti notes that Krystal Flash can be added to this pattern for more flash.

Cute-Tip

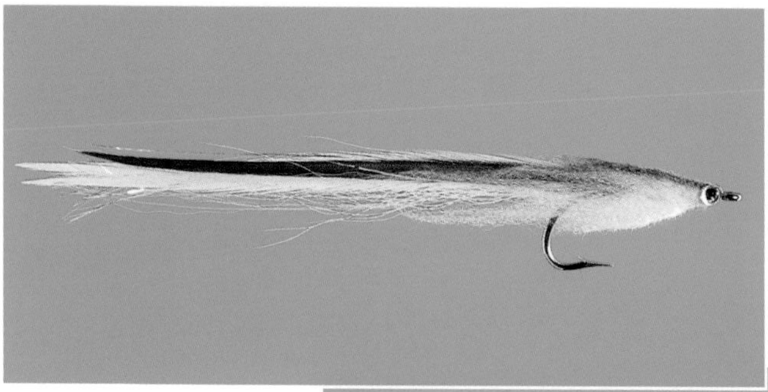

Overall length: 4 1/2" on #2 hook
Pattern type: Sand lance, sand eel
Primarily designed for: Striped bass
Also effective on: Bluefish, false albacore, bonito, weakfish
Submitted by: The Fly Hatch (Shrewsbury, New Jersey)
Originated by: David Frassinelli
Tied by: David Frassinelli

Hook: Mustad 34007, #2/0-#4
Thread: White 3/0
Wing: Two long, thin olive saddle hackles over two long, thin white saddle hackles over rainbow Polar Flash over sparse white bucktail
Body: White Glo-Bug yarn, colored green on top with permanent marker
Eyes: #1 1/2 epoxy eyes

Top view

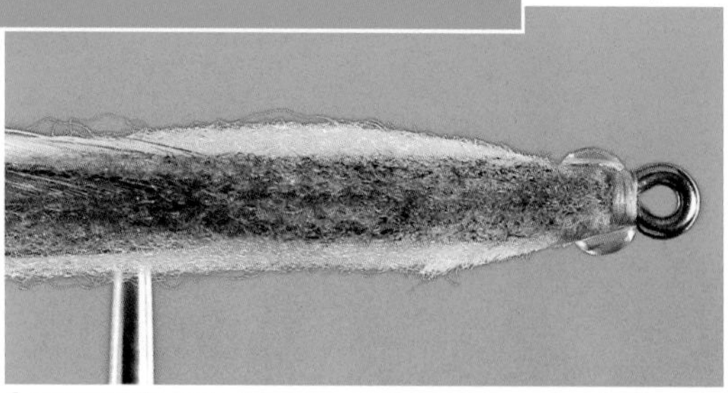

Comments: To tie body on this pattern, cut a couple of 2" lengths of Glo-Bug yarn, and pull it apart to make a clump of dubbing. Attach one small wisp of fibers at a time, stroking the previously tied fibers rearward as you add new ones. Then comb out, trim to shape, and color with marker. This fly is also very effective in chartreuse or black.

Don't Know Why

Overall length: 1" on #1/0 hook
Pattern type: General attractor
Primarily designed for: Striped bass
Also effective on: Weakfish
Submitted by: The Camp-Site (Huntington Station, New York)
Originated by: Amedeo J. Forzano
Tied by: Amedeo J. Forzano

Hook: Eagle Claw 254SS, #1/0
Thread: Fluorescent red 6/0
Body: Clear Larva Lace
Hackle: Lime green saddle feather, folded and wrapped

Comments: Amedeo J. Forzano says, "I have no idea why this fly works, but it sure does."

DRO Eel

Overall length: 7" on #2/0 hook
Pattern type: Eel
Primarily designed for: Striped bass
Also effective on: Bluefish
Submitted by: Delaware River Outfitters (Pennington, New Jersey)
Originated by: Mark Dettmar
Tied by: Mark Dettmar

Hook: Saltwater, #2/0
Thread: Black Flat waxed nylon
Tail: Loop of 30-lb. mono tied in at bend to prevent fouling of body materials
Body: Bow Tyer 2XL Black Zonker Strip over pearl Krystal Flash
Head: Chartreuse two-tone cross-cut Zonker strip, wrapped
Eyes: 5mm red 3D Molded eyes epoxied on head

Comments: Mark Dettmar says, "I designed this eel pattern for stripers in the lower Delaware River. It is most effective when fishing at night with a dead-drift technique, or long strips with a pause between. The pattern has also been very effective on the mid-Atlantic coast for stripers and bluefish."

DRO Herring

Overall length: 5 1/4" on 2/0 hook
Pattern type: Herring
Primarily designed for: Striped bass
Also effective on: Bluefish, false albacore
Submitted by: Delaware River Outfitters (Pennington, New Jersey)
Originated by: Mark Dettmar
Tied by: Mark Dettmar

Hook: Saltwater, #2/0
Thread: White Flat waxed nylon
Tail: 6 white saddle hackles flanked by chartreuse Sparkle Flash
Belly: White Aquafibers
Wing: Olive bucktail over blue Aquafibers
Gills: Red Krystal Flash
Cheeks: Mallard flank
Eyes: 5mm Prism 3D molded eyes epoxied to head

Comments: Mark Dettmar notes, "The lower Delaware River has a spring migration of herring, and when the herring start their run up the river, the striped bass follow, gorging themselves. I designed this pattern to imitate those herring. It is extremely effective when the stripers key in on the herring throughout the spring. The fly is fished with a typical cast-and-strip motion. It is also effective as a saltwater attractor pattern for stripers, bluefish, and false albacore."

Epoxy Bay Anchovy

Overall length: 3 1/4" on #2 hook
Pattern type: Anchovy
Primarily designed for: False albacore
Submitted by: North Country Outfitters (Lafayette, New Jersey)
Originated by: Unknown
Tied by: Bruce Fradl

Hook: Mustad 34007, #2
Thread: Clear mono .006"
Body: Wrap shank with 10-12 strands pearl Krystal Flash; behind eye, mount olive Craft Fur over 8 strands silver Flashabou over white Craft fur
Lateral line: 2 strands black Krystal Flash down each side; cover body materials and lateral line with 2 coats Devcon 5-minute epoxy
Throat: Red Prismacolor marker
Gills: Black Prismacolor marker
Eyes: Witchcraft #1 1/2 silver, mounted between coats of epoxy

Fly Rodders Widow

Overall length: 4 1/2" on #3/0 hook
Pattern type: Small baitfish, killie, eel
Primarily designed for: Striped bass
Also effective on: Weakfish, snook, small tarpon, speckled sea trout, bluefish, ladyfish
Submitted by: Coastal Guides Fly Shop (Brick Town, New Jersey)
Originated by: Butch Colvin
Tied by: Butch Colvin

Hook: Mustad, TMC, Siwash; #3/0-#1/0
Thread: Black Nylon 25
Tail: Black bucktail
Body: Gold Mylar tinsel
Wing: Black bucktail flanked by 3 black saddle hackles on each side
Eyes: Painted, yellow with black pupils; coat body and eyes with epoxy

Comments: Butch Colvin observes, "This pattern was created in 1965 or 1966; it was one of the first all-black streamers used in saltwater fly fishing at that time."

G&H Rock 'N' Roll

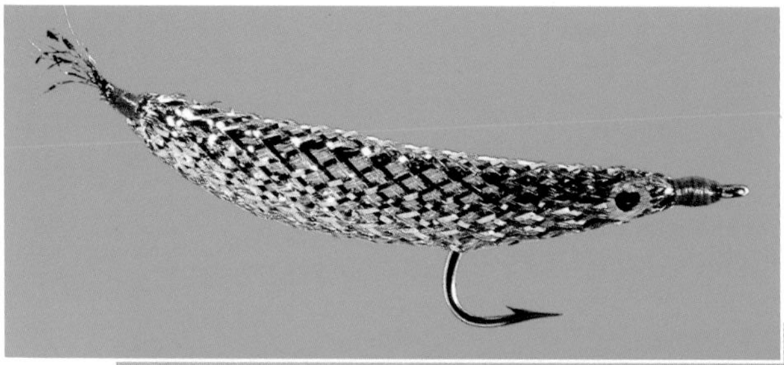

Top view

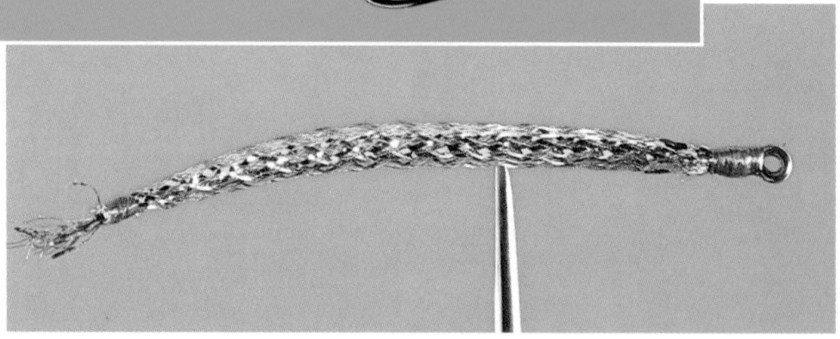

Overall length: 3" on #2/0 hook
Pattern type: Peanut bunker, moss bunker, pogie
Primarily designed for: Striped bass
Also effective on: Bluefish, false albacore, bonito
Submitted by: The Tackle Shop, Inc. (Amagansett, New York)
Originated by: Captain Harvey L. Bennet
Tied by: George Pharaoh

Hook: Mustad 34007, #4/0-#1/0
Thread: Black or gray
Tail: Green Glitter Body
Body: Gold wide Flexo tubing or 1/4" E-Z Body tubing (or silver or pearl)
Eyes: Painted, yellow with black pupils

Comments: To tie this fly (and the G&H Touch 'N' Go, below), cut a 2 1/2"-3" length of wide Flexo; thread the eye of the hook through the underside of the tubing. Put hook in vise. Pull a 5" length of Glitter Body through tubing; tie off at head, leave excess at tail. Tie off Flexo at head of fly. Reverse fly in vise. Remount thread at tail, and tie off Flexo about 1/8' from end. Hold excess Glitter Body and pull Flexo toward eye of hook, ballooning out the tubing until you have the desired body shape. Clip tail to 1/2" and cement wrappings at head and tail. Paint eyes; two or three coats will be needed to fill Flexo mesh.

G&H Touch 'N' Go

Top view

Overall length: 2 1/2" on #2 hook
Pattern type: Spearing, sand eel, or any small white bait
Primarily designed for: False albacore
Also effective on: Bluefish, striped bass, bonito
Submitted by: The Tackle Shop, Inc. (Amagansett, New York)
Originated by: Captain Harvey L. Bennett
Tied by: George Pharaoh

Hook: Mustad 34007, #1-#4
Thread: Silver, brown, or gray
Tail: Green Glitter Body
Body: Silver Flexo tubing or 1/8" EZ Body tubing (or pearl or pink tubing)
Eyes: Painted, yellow with black pupils

Comments: For details on dressing this pattern, see G&H Rock 'N' Roll, above.

Green Luster Grass Shrimp

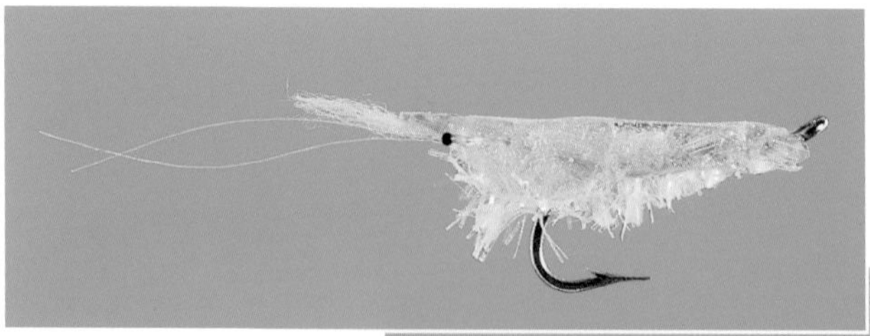

Top view

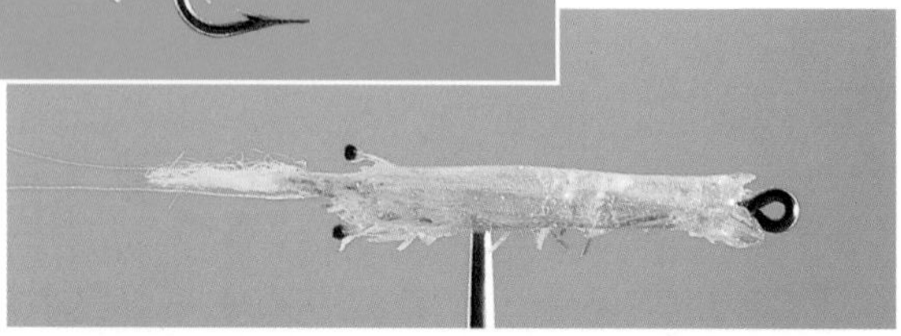

Overall length: 3" on #2 hook
Pattern type: Grass shrimp
Primarily designed for: Striped bass, white perch, weakfish
Also effective on: Redfish, snook, fluke, speckled sea trout, bluefish
Submitted by: Coastal Guides Fly Shop (Brick Town, New Jersey)
Originated by: Butch Colvin
Tied by: Butch Colvin

Hook: Mustad, Eagle Claw, TMC; #5/0-#6
Thread: Light monofilament
Body: Chartreuse Estaz (pearl for pink version)
Eyes: Monofilament, burned with ends painted black
Shellback: Prism sheet, trimmed to shape, sandwiched over body material and glued with 5-minute epoxy or Soft Coat
Mouthparts: Chartreuse wool yarn (white for pink version)
Antennae: 2 chartreuse nylon fibers (pink Krystal Flash for pink version)

Pink Luster Grass Shrimp

Green Molly

Version with chartreuse and yellow head.

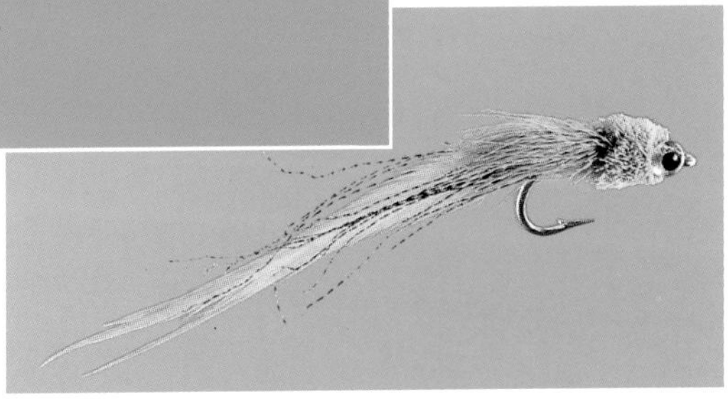

Overall length: 4 3/4" on #1/0 hook
Pattern type: General attractor
Primarily designed for: Striped bass
Also effective on: Bonito, albacore
Submitted by: Northrop's Landing (Westport, Connecticut)
Originated by: Captain Jeff Northrop
Tied by: Captain Jeff Northrop

Hook: Mustad Tarpon, #1/0
Thread: Orvis Monocord
Tail: 3 chartreuse saddle hackles and dark green Krystal Flash
Body: Chartreuse deer hair, spun and clipped (or chartreuse and yellow mixed)
Eyes: Glass doll or decoy eyes

Hester's Brown & White Epoxy Sand Eel

Top view

Comments: This pattern can also be tied in green/white, olive/white, gray/white, black/white, and chartreuse/white.

Overall length: 4" on #1 hook
Pattern type: Sand eel
Primarily designed for: Striped bass
Also effective on: Bonito, bluefish
Submitted by: Chesapeake Fly & Bait Company (Arnold, Maryland)
Originated by: Jim Hester
Tied by: Jim Hester

Hook: Mustad 34011, #2/0-#1
Thread: Monofilament thread
Tail: Brown ostrich herl over white ostrich herl flanked by 4-6 strands holographic Mylar per side
Underbody: Small pearl Mylar tubing
Overbody: Small pearl E-Z Body tubing, back colored with brown permanent marker, gills with red marker, coated with epoxy
Eyes: Small plated barbell eyes, painted with black pupils, coated with epoxy

Hester's Brown Sea Worm

Overall length: 5" on #2/0 hook
Pattern type: Various aquatic worms
Primarily designed for: Striped bass
Also effective on: Bonito, bluefish, sea trout, redfish, dolphin, flounder, croaker
Submitted by: Chesapeake Fly & Bait Company (Arnold, Maryland)
Originated by: Jim Hester
Tied by: Jim Hester

Hook: Any saltwater, #4/0-#2/0; weighted with several wraps .020" lead wire
Thread: Fire orange Danville Flat waxed nylon
Tail: 3-4 pairs natural brown or furnace saddle hackle, flanked by pearl Flashabou
Body: Amber Swannundaze over fire orange tying thread to cover lead wire
Hackle: Natural brown saddle hackle
Head: Fire orange tying thread coated with epoxy

Hester's Chartreuse Striper Streamer

Overall length: 4 3/4" on #3/0 hook
Pattern type: Attractor
Primarily designed for: Striped bass
Also effective on: Bluefish
Submitted by: Chesapeake Fly & Bait Company (Arnold, Maryland)
Originated by: Jim Hester
Tied by: Jim Hester

Hook: Mustad 34007, #4/0-#1/0
Thread: Chartreuse Danville Flat waxed nylon
Tail: 3 pairs chartreuse neck hackles, tied splayed, over white bucktail
Body: Chartreuse saddle hackle, palmered thickly on shank
Head: Pearlescent chartreuse Cactus Chenille, clipped to shape and coated with epoxy
Eyes: Plastic

Top view

Comments: This fly can be tied in a number of other colors—black, hot pink, white, purple, and yellow. All have white bucktail in the tail except the black version, which can be tied with either white or black bucktail. The all black version is primarily for night fishing; on this pattern, glow-in-the-dark glitter can be added to the epoxy used on the fly head.

Hester's Floating Baitfish

Overall length: 4 1/2" on #2/0 hook
Pattern type: Various baitfish: shad, herring, alewife, menhaden
Primarily designed for: Striped bass
Also effective on: Sea trout, redfish, snook, bluefish
Submitted by: Chesapeake Fly & Bait Company (Arnold, Maryland)
Originated by: Jim Hester
Tied by: Jim Hester

Hook: Any saltwater, #4/0-#2/0
Thread: Fire orange Danville Flat waxed nylon
Weed guard (optional): 30-lb. Mason hard nylon
Tail: 3 pairs white saddle or neck hackles over white bucktail flank by 6 strands holographic Mylar per side
Body: Pearl Cactus Chenille
Shellback: White 6mm closed-cell foam strip
Hackle: 2-3 wraps red saddle or neck hackle
Eyes: 10mm doll eyes

Top view

Comments: The tail on this pattern is tied with the hackle feathers splayed outward. After dressing the tail, affix the end of the foam strip 1/4" behind the hook eye and bind the foam down the entire length of the shank. Tie in the Cactus Chenille at the rear, and wrap forward, ending 5/16" behind eye. Tie in and wrap the red hackles. Clip the chenille body flat along the top. Place few drops of Super Glue atop the clipped chenille, and bring the foam forward, pressing against the glue. Bind down the foam just behind the hook eye. Flatten and tie in the front of the weed guard (if used). Super glue the doll eyes to the sides of the head, covering the thread wraps on the foam as well. Finish the head by adding epoxy to the "valley" formed between the doll eyes.

Lefco Squid

Overall length: 6" on #4/0 hook
Pattern type: Squid
Primarily designed for: Tuna
Also effective on: Dolphin, rockfish, bonito, bluefish, sea trout
Submitted by: Lead Eyes Fly Company (Ocean City, Maryland)
Originated by: Captain Tim Tanis
Tied by: Captain Tim Tanis

Hook: Mustad 34007 or Mustad 34011, #4/0-#1/0
Thread: Danville Fine Monofilament
Long tentacles: 4-6 long, curved white saddle hackles, mixed with 4-6 strands pink (or red) Krystal Flash
Short tentacles: 10-12 white saddle hackles
Eyes: 1/2"- 3/8" Witch Stix 3-D Molded Epoxy Eyes, red (silver or chartreuse)
Body: White Crystal Chenille
Collar: Pearl Flashabou over white bucktail

Top view

Comments: Captain Tanis explains, "We fish this fly on 8-weight to 13-weight rods with 225 grain to 650 grain lines. Let the fly sink to the desired depth, then use a fast, stop-and-go strip retrieve." The fly was designed for the mid-Atlantic area around Ocean City, Maryland.

Mad Gails Mullet

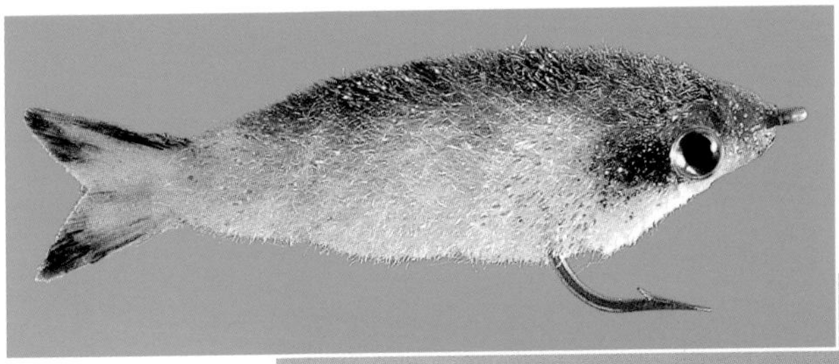

Top view

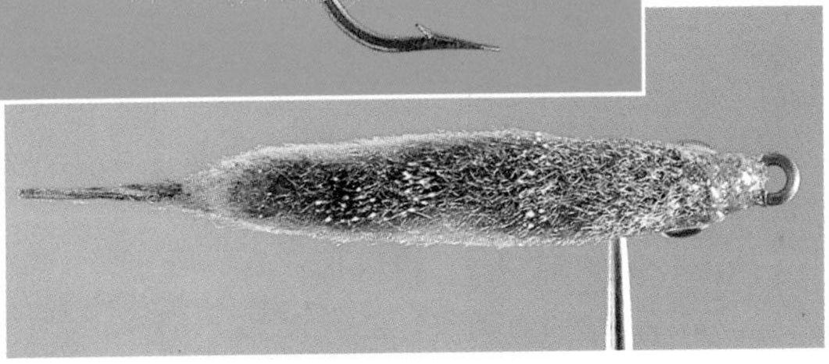

Overall length: 2 1/2" on #1/0 hook
Pattern type: Mullet
Primarily designed for: Striped bass, bluefish
Also effective on: Weakfish, snook, tarpon, speckled sea trout, fluke, ladyfish
Submitted by: Coastal Guides Fly Shop (Brick Town, New Jersey)
Originated by: Butch Colvin
Tied by: Butch Colvin

Hook: Eagle Claw, TMC, Siwash, #1/0 or to match natural
Thread: Monofilament
Tail: White Sea Fibre (or Sea Hair or Polafibre) glued and trimmed to shape, colored with gray permanent marker
Body: White Sea Hair, colored on top with gray permanent marker
Gill covers: Pearl Krystal Flash; small amount of gold glitter glued behind eye, colored over top with blue permanent marker
Eyes: 3-D Molded Stick-on eyes, silver

The Magician

Yellow version

Overall length: 4 1/2" on #1/0 hook
Pattern type: Silverside, mullet, baitfish
Primarily designed for: Striped bass
Also effective on: Weakfish, bluefish, fluke, speckled sea trout, redfish, tarpon, and other species
Submitted by: Coastal Guides Fly Shop (Brick Town, New Jersey)
Originated by: Butch Colvin
Tied by: Butch Colvin

Comments: "This fly was created in 1964," notes Butch Colvin, "Very popular, then and now."

Hook: Eagle Claw, TMC, Siwash; #3/0-#1/0
Thread: White nylon, medium
Tail: White marabou (yellow for yellow version)
Body: White chenille (yellow for yellow version)
Wing: White bucktail (yellow bucktail for yellow version) flanked by 2 white saddle hackles (yellow for yellow version) on each side, flanked by one badger hackle per side
Shoulders: Jungle cock eye tied over teal flank feather; then cemented
Head: Tying thread coated with green iridescent pearl paint
Eyes: Stick-on eyes, gold with black pupils (or painted, as shown on yellow version, yellow with black pupil)

Mega Clouser (Blue/Green)

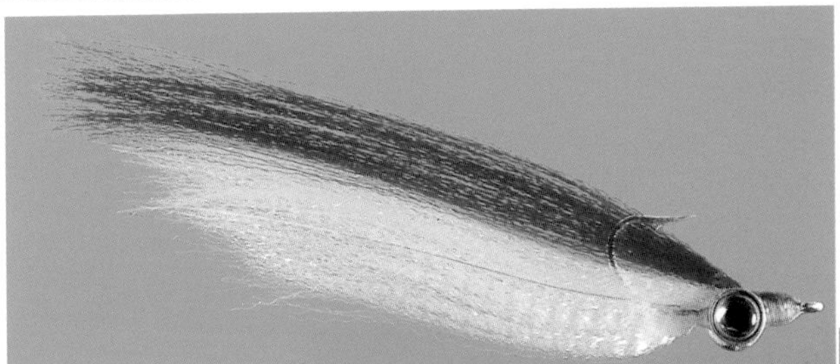

Top view

Overall length: 6 1/2" on #3/0 hook
Pattern type: General attractor
Primarily designed for: Dolphin
Also effective on: Amberjack, cobia, striped bass, bluefish, black drum, flounder, speckled sea trout, billfish
Submitted by: Angler's Lab Outfitters (Virginia Beach, Virginia)
Originated by: Ron Russell variation of Bob Clouser design
Tied by: Ron Russell

Hook: Mustad 34007, #4/0-#1/0
Thread: White Flat waxed nylon
Eyes: Large Spirit River Deep See Aluminum Barbell with silver 3-D Molded Stick-on eyes inserts
Wing: Blue Super Hair over chartreuse Super Hair over pearl Flashabou, tied behind hook eye
Belly: White Super Hair
Head: Tying thread colored on top with blue Prisma Pen to match wing material; coated with 5-minute epoxy

Mega Clouser
(Chartreuse/White)

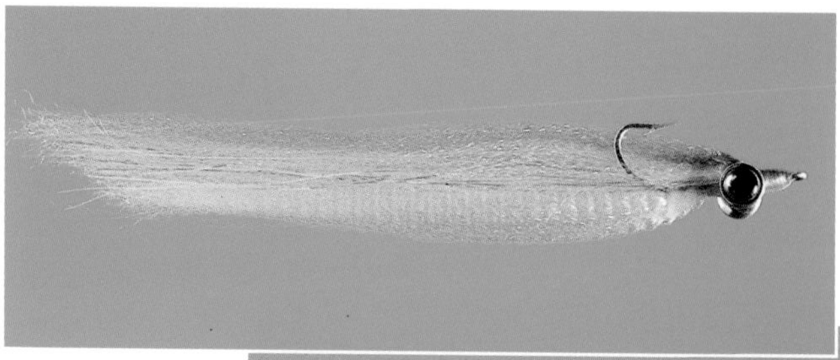

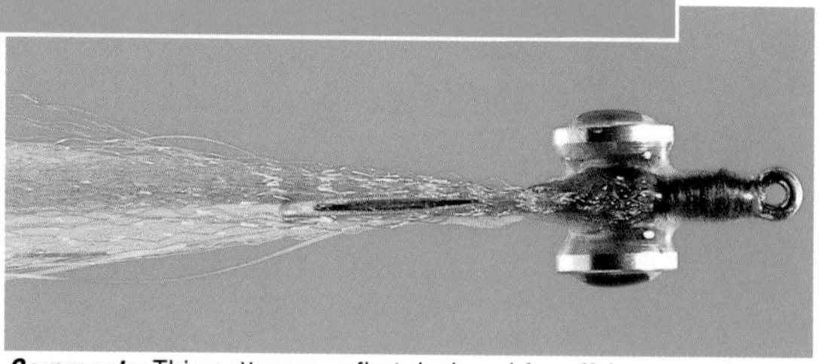

Top view

Overall length: 7 1/2" on #3/0 hook
Pattern type: Mullet, menhaden, herring
Primarily designed for: Billfish
Also effective on: Tuna, amberjack, cobia, striped bass, black drum, flounder
Submitted by: Angler's Lab Outfitters (Virginia Beach, Virginia)
Originated by: Pete Bregant version of Bob Clouser design
Tied by: Pete Bregant

Hook: Mustad 34007, #4/0-#1/0
Thread: White Flat waxed nylon
Wing: Light olive Super Hair over chartreuse Super Hair over pearl Flashabou
Belly: White Super Hair
Eyes: Large Spirit River Deep See Aluminum Eyes with silver 3-D Molded Stick-on eyes inserts
Head: White tying thread colored olive on top with Prisma Pen to match wing color; coated with 5-minute epoxy

Comments: This pattern was first designed for offshore species such as bluefin tuna, but proved equally effective on inshore species. When applying epoxy to the head, apply a small amount to the base of the wing and belly materials just behind the eyes; then squeeze the fibers flat to widen the fly profile.

Mega Clouser (White)

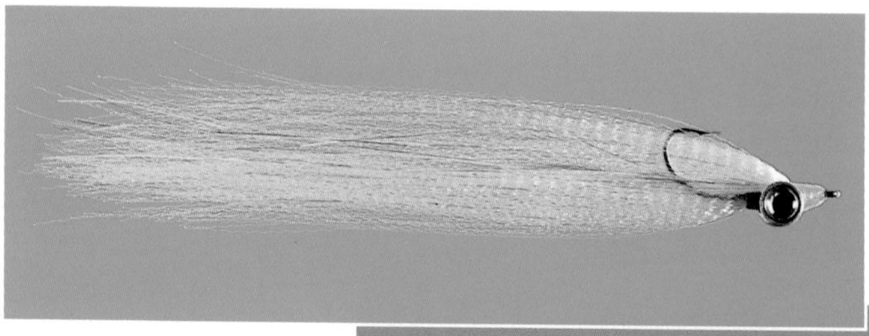

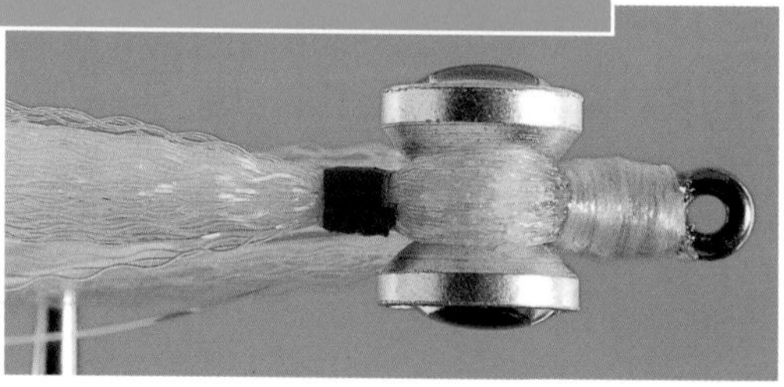

Bottom view

Overall length: 7" on #3/0 hook
Pattern type: General attractor
Primarily designed for: Dolphin
Also effective on: Cobia, striped bass, bluefish, black drum, flounder, speckled sea trout, billfish
Submitted by: Angler's Lab Outfitters (Virginia Beach, Virginia)
Originated by: Ron Russell version of Bob Clouser design
Tied by: Ron Russell

Hook: Mustad 34007, #4/0-#1/0
Thread: White Flat waxed nylon
Wing: White Super Hair over pearl Flashabou
Belly: White Super Hair
Gills: Band of red tying thread
Eyes: Medium Spirit River Deep See Aluminum Eyes with silver 3-D Molded Stick-on eyes inserts
Head: Tying thread coated with 5-minute epoxy

Mobjack Shrimp (Chartreuse)

Overall length: 2 1/4" on #4 hook
Pattern type: Grass shrimp
Primarily designed for: Speckled sea trout
Also effective on: Atlantic croaker
Submitted by: Severn Wharf Custom Rods (Gloucester Point, Virginia)
Originated by: Neil Drumheller
Tied by: Neil Drumheller

Hook: Eagle Claw L067FS Lazer Sharp, #4
Thread: Chartreuse 3/0
Antennae: Chartreuse Krystal Flash and 2 peacock herls
Eyes: Extra-small (5/32") plated barbell eyes
Body: Chartreuse Estaz
Tail: Chartreuse Ultra Hair

Mobjack Shrimp (White)

Overall length: 2 1/4" on #4 hook
Pattern type: Grass shrimp
Primarily designed for: Speckled sea trout
Also effective on: Atlantic croaker
Submitted by: Severn Wharf Custom Rods (Gloucester Point, Virginia)
Originated by: Neil Drumheller
Tied by: Neil Drumheller

Hook: Eagle Claw L067FS Lazer Sharp, #4
Thread: White 3/0
Antennae: White FisHair and 2 peacock herls
Eyes: Extra-small (5/32") plated barbell eyes
Body: White Estaz
Tail: White FisHair

Neil's Sparse Silverside

Overall length: 2 3/4" on #2 hook
Pattern type: Silverside minnow
Primarily designed for: Speckled sea trout
Also effective on: Striped bass
Submitted by: Severn Wharf Custom Rods (Gloucester Point, Virginia)
Originated by: Neil Drumheller
Tied by: Neil Drumheller

Hook: Mustad 34011, #2
Thread: White 3/0
Body: Flat silver Mylar tinsel, medium
Wing: Peacock herl over silver Krystal Flash over white Ultra Hair
Eyes: Extra-small (5/32") plated barbell eyes

Comments: The plated eyes and sparse tie, says Neil Drumheller, produce more strikes. Fish it in or on the edge of grass beds with a slow retrieve.

Punk Blonde

Overall length: 4" on #2/0 hook
Pattern type: Attractor
Primarily designed for: Striped bass
Also effective on: Bluefish, sea trout, redfish
Submitted by: Chesapeake Fly & Bait Company (Arnold, Maryland)
Originated by: Jim Hester
Tied by: Jim Hester

Hook: Mustad 34007 or Mustad 3407, #3/0-#1/0
Thread: Hot pink Danville Depth Ray Nylon
Tail: Hot pink bucktail over fluorescent chartreuse bucktail
Body: Silver Mylar tinsel
Wing: Purple bucktail over fluorescent blue bucktail flanked by 6-10 strands holographic Mylar per side
Head: Tying thread coated with epoxy
Eyes: Painted, white with black pupils

Comments: This fly is tied in the Joe Brooks Blonde style.

Rube's Anchovy

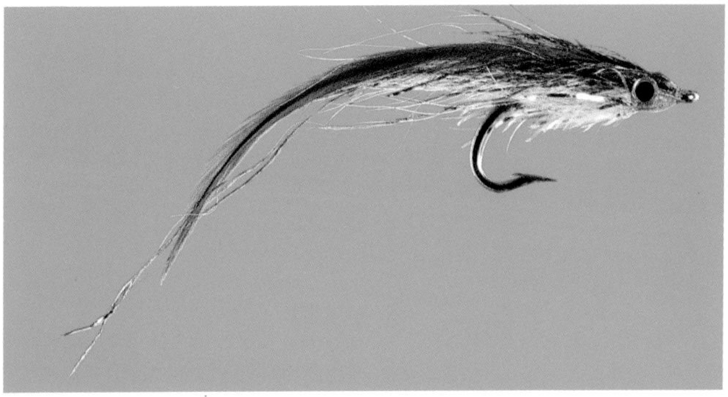

Overall length: 3 1/4" on #6 hook
Pattern type: Anchovy
Primarily designed for: Most predatory species
Submitted by: Housatonic River Outfitters, Inc. (West Cornwall, Connecticut)
Originated by: Don Rubenstein
Tied by: Don Rubenstein

Hook: Partridge Sea Prince, #6
Thread: Clear Mono
Body: Brown bucktail over two brown saddle hackles tied flat over brown bucktail over copper Tiewell over white bucktail
Belly: Pearl green Tiewell
Head: Epoxy
Eyes: #2 Stick-on eyes, silver with black pupils

Rube's Blushing Wide Fly

Top view

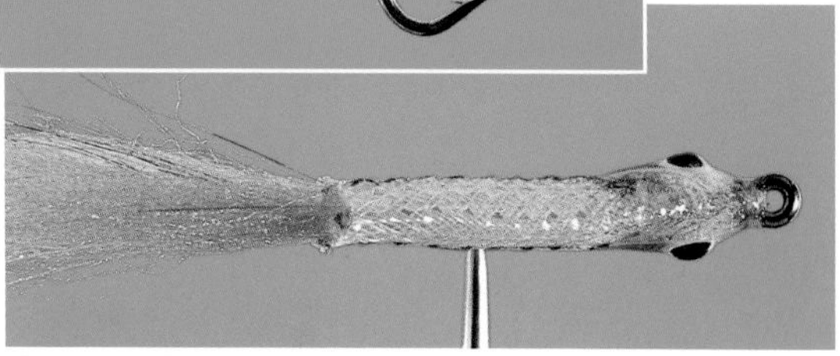

Overall length: 4 1/4" on #1/0 hook
Pattern type: Baitfish
Primarily designed for: Striped bass
Also effective on: Bluefish
Submitted by: Housatonic River Outfitters, Inc. (West Cornwall, Connecticut)
Originated by: Don Rubenstein
Tied by: Don Rubenstein

Hook: Gamakatsu SL11-3H or similar hook, #1/0
Thread: Clear Mono
Wing: Cap's Wing Fiber, chartreuse over white
Gills: Pearl red Angel Hair
Body: Large pearl tubing
Gill cover and lateral line: Black permanent marker
Eyes: Plastic doll eyes coated with epoxy

Comments: Don Rubenstein observes, "This is a great striper and bluefish fly that lights up in the water and gets great action from the wing fibers. A very thin coat of epoxy can be applied to the body tubing to toughen it for blues."

Rube's Wounded Baby Bunker

Front view: showing dressing offset at 45-degree angle.

Overall length: 2 3/4" on #1 hook
Pattern type: Baby bunker or butterfish
Primarily designed for: Bonito
Submitted by: Housatonic River Outfitters, Inc. (West Cornwall, Connecticut)
Originated by: Don Rubenstein
Tied by: Don Rubenstein

Hook: Gamakatsu SL11-3H, #1
Thread: Clear Mono
Body: Widows Web mixed with Angel Hair (pearl, green, and silver); top: gray, side: lavender, belly: white; tied in bunches staggered along shank, combed and trimmed
Lateral line: Pink Fluorofiber
Gills: Pearl red Angel Hair or Lite Brite
Eyes: Plastic doll eyes glued on with Goop

Comments: Don Rubenstein explains, "All body fibers are tied and secured with Zap-A-Gap on the hook at a 45-degree angle. This makes the fly land on its side and roll like a wounded fish. A heavy hook like the SL11-3H is needed to roll the fly on its side. The fly is trimmed to shape after combing and can be trimmed on the water to a smaller size if needed to match the natural baitfish."

Saltwater Grub

Overall length: 4 1/2" on #2/0 hook
Pattern type: Attractor
Primarily designed for: Striped bass
Also effective on: Bluefish, sea trout, redfish, snook
Submitted by: Chesapeake Fly & Bait Company (Arnold, Maryland)
Originated by: Jim Hester
Tied by: Jim Hester

Hook: Eagle Claw 254 CAT or Eagle Claw 254N, #4/0-#2/0
Thread: Fire orange Danville Depth Ray Nylon
Tail: Several purple marabou feathers flanked by holographic Mylar
Body: Pearlescent purple Cactus Chenille
Head: Tying thread coated with epoxy
Eyes: Painted, white with black pupils
Weed guard (optional): 30-lb. hard Mason nylon

Comments: This fly was designed to be fished like the plastic grubs used by spin fishermen. It is especially good in late fall when water clarity is improved. Other favorite color combinations are black with red head, black with chartreuse head, white with red head, white with white head, chartreuse with red head, chartreuse with chartreuse head, and purple with red head.

Sand Crab

Overall length: 2" on #2/0 hook
Pattern type: Sand crab (mole crab)
Primarily designed for: Striped bass
Also effective on: Weakfish, Atlantic king fish, fluke
Submitted by: Coastal Guides Fly Shop (Brick Town, New Jersey)
Originated by: Butch Colvin
Tied by: Butch Colvin

Hook: TMC, Siwash, #3/0-#1/0
Thread: Heavy rod-winding nylon thread
Body: Deer hair, spun and clipped
Legs: Deer hair from body coated with Duco cement or airplane glue

Comments: Butch Colvin explains, "I designed this fly after snorkeling behind the backwash of the surf along our beach front in New Jersey. I saw striped bass feeding on sand crabs, so I tied this pattern and it proved successful. It's fished very much like nymph fishing—lots of patience and practice. This was the first crab used at that time—1966—in saltwater fly rodding."

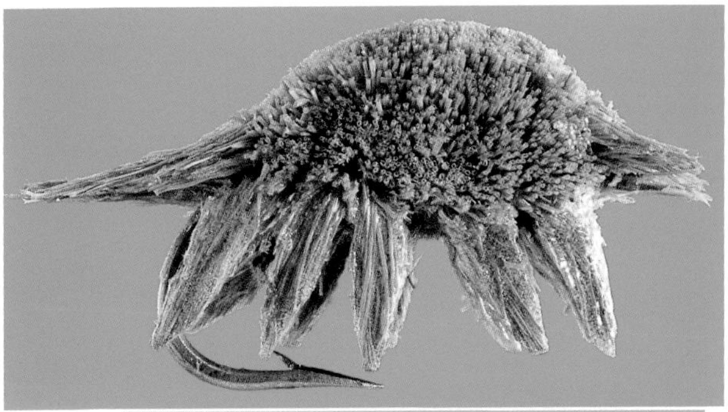

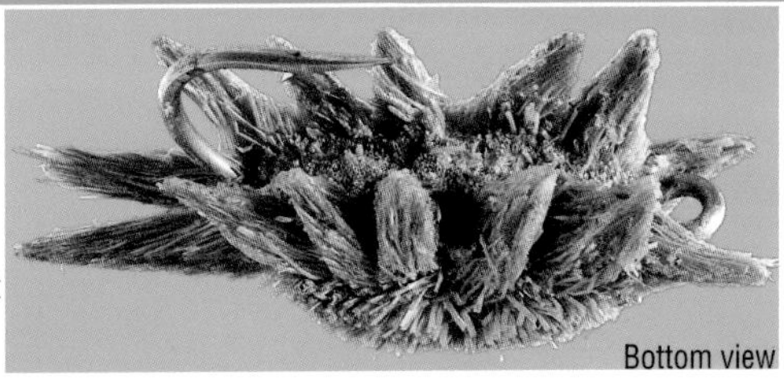

Bottom view

Shenk's Pearly Killer

Overall length: 2 1/2" on #2 hook
Pattern type: General attractor, minnow
Primarily designed for: Striped bass
Submitted by: South Mountain Custom Rod & Tackle (Lebanon, Pennsylvania)
Originated by: David R. Shenk
Tied by: David R. Shenk

Hook: Mustad 3665A or TMC 300, #6-#14
Thread: Black
Tail: Black FisHair
Body: White Sparkle Antron
Wing: Pearl Krystal Flash over black FisHair, flanked by 1 mallard breast feather on each side
Head: Fine lead wire overwrapped with white rod-winding thread, covered with 3 coats white vinyl jig enamel
Eyes (optional): Stick-on eyes, red with black pupils, coated with 5-minute epoxy

Wing on near side raised to show underwing and body.

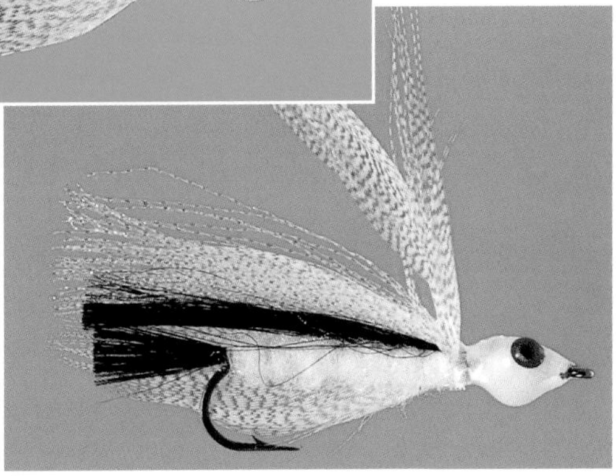

Comments: Originally designed as a trout pattern, this fly has proven effective on a variety of species.

Slider Bug

Overall length: 7 1/4" on #1/0 hook; 4 3/4" on #2 hook
Pattern type: Baitfish
Primarily designed for: Striped bass
Also effective on: Bluefish, false albacore, any piscivorous species
Submitted by: Delaware River Anglers (Willow Grove, Pennsylvania)
Originated by: Ken Schwam
Tied by: Ken Schwam

Hook: Mustad 34011, #1/0-#4
Thread: Black UNI 6/0 for tail; black size A flat waxed nylon for head (white threads for white version)
Tail: 6-10 black saddle feathers (white for white version) tied back-to-back, Deceiver style, topped with pearl Flashabou (silver Flashabou for white version)
Collar: Hair tips from spun body over 1-2 two webby saddle hackles wrapped as collar
Head: Black deer hair, spun and clipped

Comments: "This fly," explains Ken Schwam, "imitates a crippled or wounded baitfish. It is deadly for swirling stripers or as a searching pattern. The best colors are black, white, yellow, chartreuse, and light pink. My favorites are a #2 yellow and a #1/0 black. It is best fished slowly with a steady two-hand retrieve. Sometimes I put floatant on the fly. When tying this pattern, make sure that the deer-hair body head does not extend any farther back than the hook point."

Spunks Bunks Silver Dollar

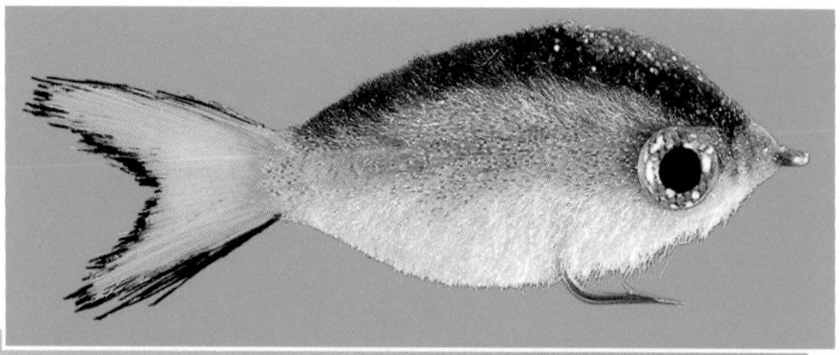

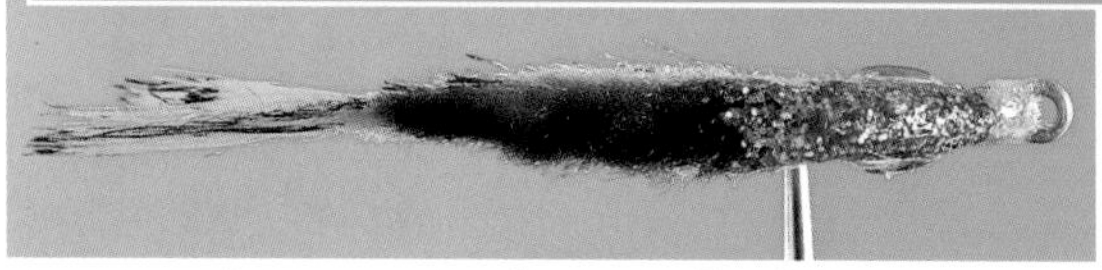

Overall length: 3 1/4" on #1/0 hook
Pattern type: Small bunker
Primarily designed for: Striped bass
Also effective on: Large weakfish, tarpon, speckled sea trout, redfish, bluefish, and many saltwater species
Submitted by: Coastal Guides Fly Shop (Brick Town, New Jersey)
Originated by: Butch Colvin
Tied by: Butch Colvin

Hook: Eagle Claw, TMC, Siwash, #1/0
Thread: Medium monofilament
Tail: Yellow Polafibre or Sea Hair, edged with black permanent marker
Back: Pink Sea Hair, colored on back with purple permanent marker, topped on front with silicone mixed with violet glitter
Belly: White Sea Hair
Lateral line: Pearl Krystal Flash
Eyes: 3-D Molded Stick-on eyes, prizma silver

Comments: This fly is fished by alternating 3 quick strips with pauses to imitate a wounded baitfish.

Spunks Bunks Swimmer

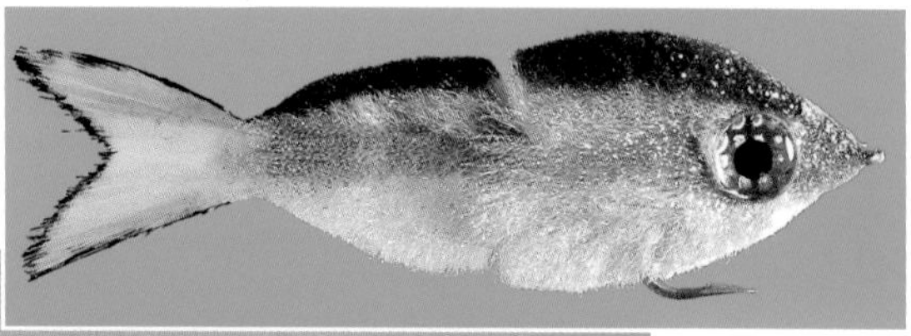

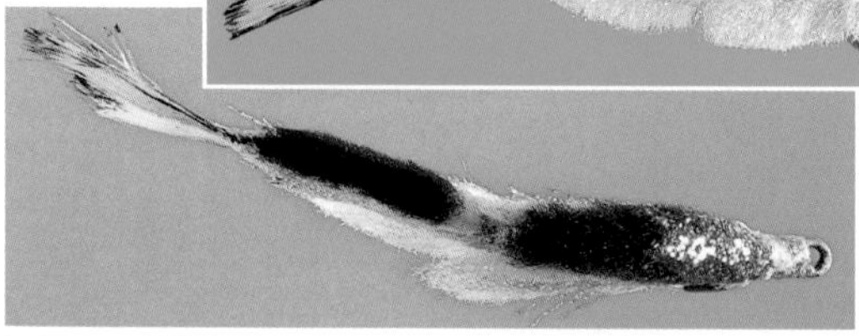

Top view showing articulated body.

Overall length: 4 1/2" on #3/0 hook
Pattern type: Moss bunker
Primarily designed for: Large striped bass
Also effective on: Bluefish, tarpon, tuna, billfish, sharks
Submitted by: Coastal Guides Fly Shop (Brick Town, New Jersey)
Originated by: Butch Colvin
Tied by: Butch Colvin

Hook: Eagle Claw, TMC Siwash; #9/0-#1/0
Thread: Medium monofilament
Body extension: Doubled length of heavy monofilament; loop at front
Wiggle hinge: Doubled length of heavy monofilament lashed to hook shank; loop at rear
Tail: White Sea Hair or Polafibre, colored with yellow and black permanent markers
Back: Pink Sea Hair, colored on back with purple permanent marker, topped on front with silicone mixed with violet glitter
Belly: White Sea Hair
Lateral line: Pearl Krystal Flash tied in then glued to sides on body extension; tied in then glued beneath eye on front of body
Eyes: 3-D Molded Stick-on eyes, prizma silver
Head: Silicone mixed with violet glitter

Detail of wiggle hinge.

Super Mullet

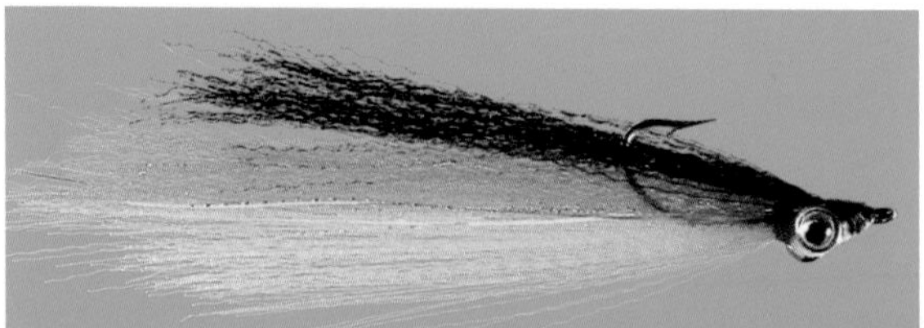

Bottom view

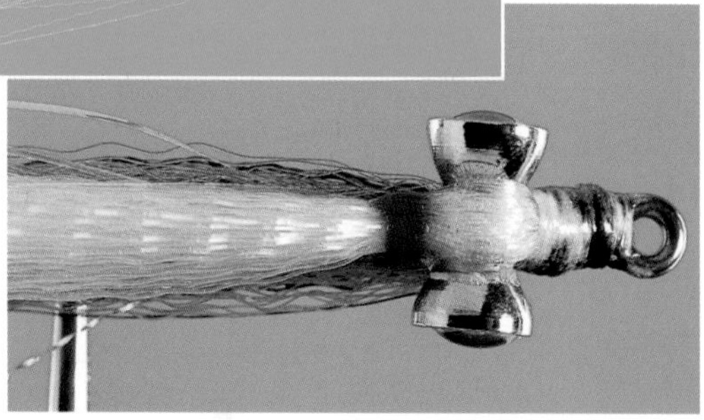

Overall length: 5" on #2/0 hook
Pattern type: Mullet
Primarily designed for: Striped bass
Also effective on: Black drum, redfish, bluefish, speckled sea trout, cobia
Submitted by: Angler's Lab Outfitters (Virginia Beach, Virginia)
Originated by: Ron Russell version of Bob Clouser design
Tied by: Ron Russell

Hook: Mustad 34007, #2/0-#4
Thread: White Flat waxed nylon
Wing: Black Super Hair over gray Super Hair over pearl Flashabou
Belly: White Super Hair over silver Krystal Flash
Gills: Band of red Flat waxed nylon
Eyes: Small Spirit River Deep See Aluminum Eyes with silver 3-D Molded Stick-on eyes inserts
Head: White tying thread colored black on top with permanent marker; coated with 5-minute epoxy

Comments: Tyer Ron Russell notes that he took this color scheme from the Black Back Windcheater lure.

Super Sea-Ducer

Overall length: 4 3/4" on #2/0 hook
Pattern type: Attractor
Primarily designed for: Striped bass
Also effective on: Snook, sea trout, redfish, cobia, dolphin, bluefish, tarpon
Submitted by: Chesapeake Fly & Bait Company (Arnold, Maryland)
Originated by: Jim Hester adaptation of Sea-Ducer
Tied by: Jim Hester

Hook: Mustad 34007 or other standard saltwater hook, #4/0-#2
Thread: Yellow Danville 3/0 Monocord or Flat waxed nylon
Tail: 5 pairs yellow neck or saddle hackles, tied splayed; flanked by 6 strands holographic Mylar per side
Body: Yellow pearlescent Cactus Chenille
Ribbing: Yellow hackle, palmered over body
Collar: Red hackle
Eyes: Plastic, epoxied in place
Head: Epoxy with glitter mixed in
Weed guard (optional): 30-lb. hard Mason nylon

Bottom view

Comments: This modified Sea-Ducer is more durable than the original and is attractive to many fish species. Other favorite colors include white with red collar, black with orange collar, chartreuse with red collar. It can also be tied inverted by adding barbell eyes.

Super Streamer (Anchovy Variation)

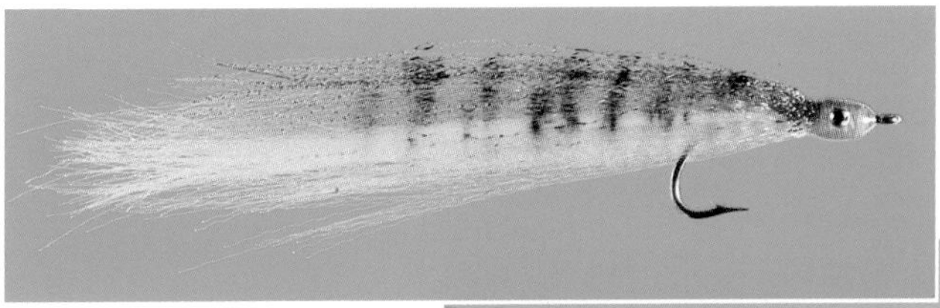

Overall length: 5 1/4" on #2/0 hook
Pattern type: Baitfish
Primarily designed for: Striped bass
Also effective on: False albacore, redfish, black drum, sea trout, bluefish
Submitted by: Angler's Lab Outfitters (Virginia Beach, Virginia)
Originated by: Steve Burton
Tied by: Steve Burton

Top view

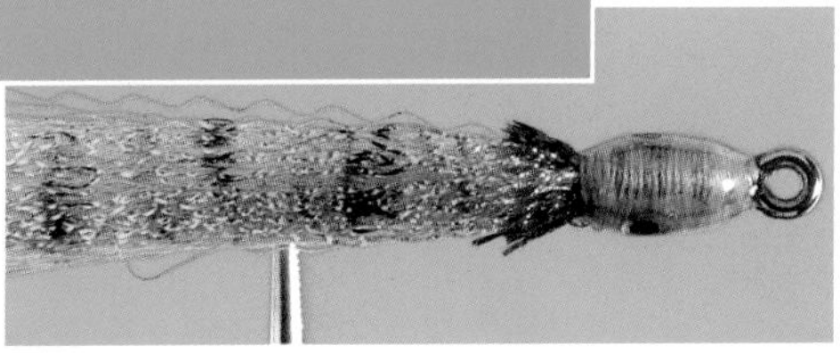

Hook: Mustad 34007, #2/0
Thread: White Flat waxed nylon
Wing: Olive Krystal Flash over olive Super Hair, over chartreuse Super Hair over pearl Flashabou over white `Super Hair; vertical bars added with black permanent marker
Gills: Red Krystal Flash
Head: Tying thread colored olive on top to match wing color
Eyes: Stick-on eyes, gold with black pupils; head and eyes coated with 5-minute epoxy

Super Streamer (Chartreuse/White)

Overall length: 4 3/4" on #2/0 hook
Pattern type: Baitfish
Primarily designed for: Striped bass
Also effective on: Redfish, black drum, bluefish, sea trout
Submitted by: Angler's Lab Outfitters (Virginia Beach, Virginia)
Originated by: Steve Burton
Tied by: Steve Burton

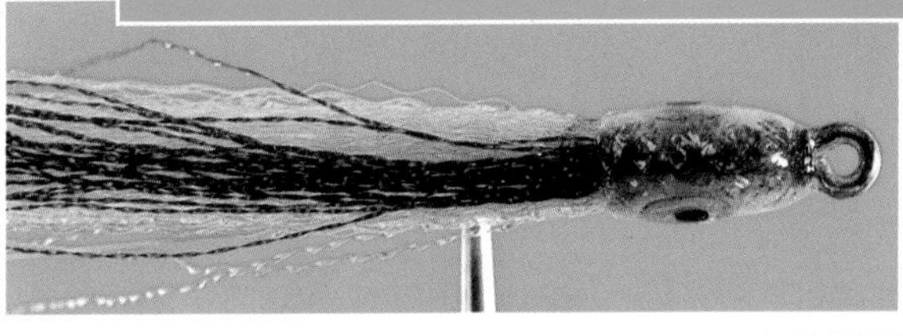

Top view

Hook: Mustad 7766, #2/0
Thread: White Danville Flat waxed nylon
Wing: Peacock Krystal Flash over olive Super Hair over chartreuse Super Hair over pearl Krystal Flash over chartreuse Flashabou (substitute chartreuse Krystal Flash for alternate version) over white Super Hair
Belly: White Super Hair
Gills (for alternate version): Red Krystal Flash
Head: Pearl EZ Body Braid, medium; coated with epoxy
Eyes: 5/16"Stick-on eyes, silver; coated with epoxy

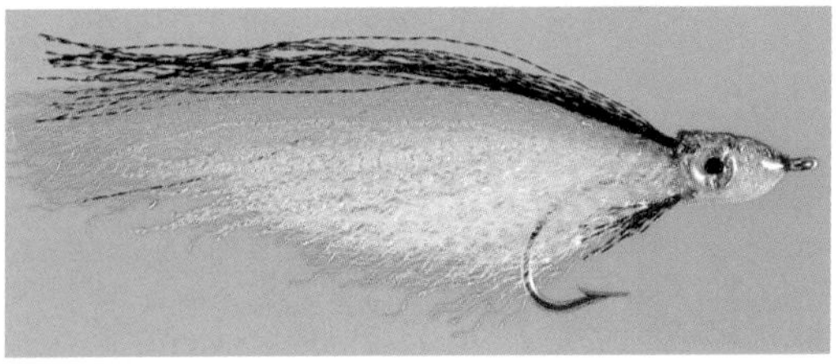

Version using chartreuse Krystal Flash in wing and red Krystal Flash gills.

Super Streamer (Sea Foam/Pink)

Overall length: 5 3/4" on #1/0 hook
Pattern type: Baitfish
Primarily designed for: Striped bass
Also effective on: Redfish, black drum, bluefish, speckled sea trout
Submitted by: Angler's Lab Outfitters (Virginia Beach, Virginia)
Originated by: Steve Burton
Tied by: Steve Burton

Hook: Mustad 34007, #1/0
Thread: White Danville Flat waxed nylon
Wing: Peacock Krystal Flash over sea foam Super Hair over pink Super Hair over white Super Hair over pearl Krystal Flash
Belly: White Super Hair
Gills: Band of red tying thread
Eyes: 1/8" prismatic Stick-on eyes
Head: 5-minute epoxy

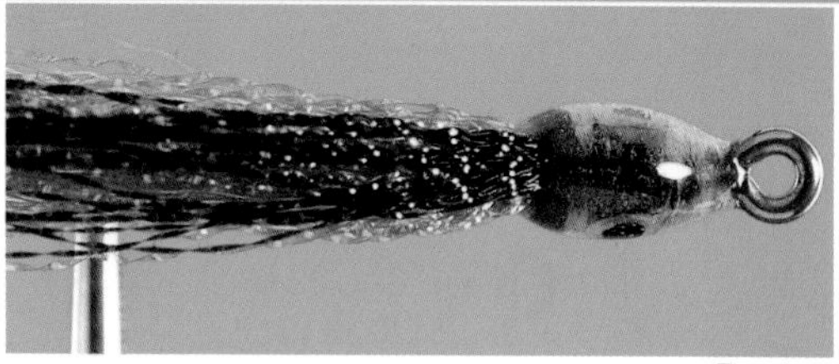

Top view

Sweet Cheeks

Overall length: 3 3/4" on #1/0 hook
Pattern type: Bay anchovy
Primarily designed for: Striped bass
Also effective on: Bluefish, false albacore
Submitted by: The Fly Hatch (Shrewsbury, New Jersey)
Originated by: David Frassinelli
Tied by: David Frassinelli

Bottom view

Hook: Mustad 34007, #2/0-#2
Thread: White 3/0
Tail: Pearl blue Polar Flash over white bucktail
Body: Red Bill's Bodi-Braid
Wing: Root beer bucktail over tan bucktail, flanked by frayed red braid from body
Cheeks: Small Fry Side Lites
Topping: Brown bucktail
Eyes: Mylar; eyes, cheeks, and head coated in Softex

Comments: On this pattern, the brown bucktail topping is tied in after the cheeks. David Frassinelli points out that the cheek material is easier to cut without fraying if it is first coated with Softex.

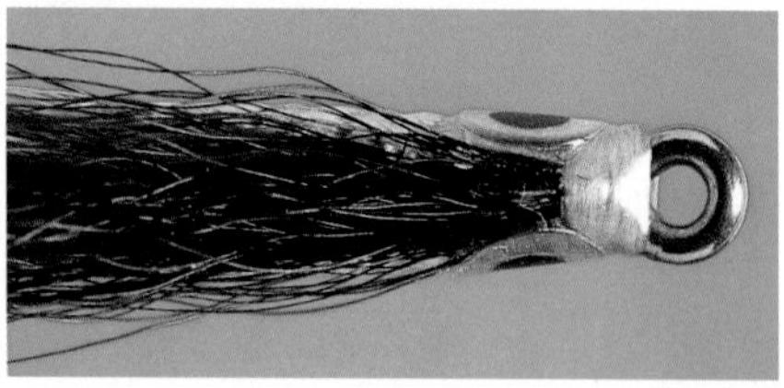

Top view

Yak Attack

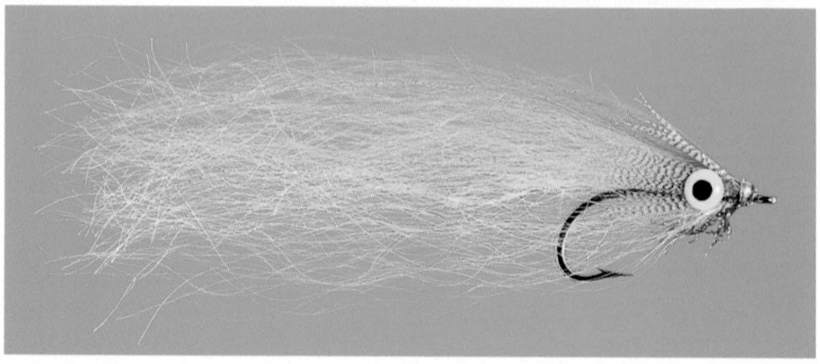

Overall length: 5" on #2/0 hook
Pattern type: Generic baitfish imitation
Primarily designed for: Striped bass
Also effective on: Nearly all saltwater game fish
Submitted by: Delaware River Anglers (Willow Grove, Pennsylvania)
Originated by: Ken Schwam
Tied by: Ken Schwam

Comments: This fly is simple to tie and durable; it casts well for its size. It can be tied in a variety of colors. Delaware River Anglers sells a materials/ instruction kit for this pattern.

Hook: Mustad 34007, #2/0
Thread: White UNI 6/0
Wing: Blue yak hair over pearl Flashabou over light green yak hair over pearl Flashabou
Belly: White yak hair
Cheeks: Mallard flank
Gills: Red Krystal Flash
Eyes: Yellow Stick-on eyes attached with clear silicone caulk

CHAPTER 3

Gulf States and Florida

Florida – Georgia – Louisiana – Texas

Algal Bloom

Overall length: 2 1/2" on #2 hook
Pattern type: Shrimp
Primarily designed for: Bonefish
Submitted by: Key West Angler (Key West, Florida)
Originated by: John O'Hearn and Bryan Yates
Tied by: John O'Hearn

Hook: Partridge Sea Prince, #2-#4
Thread: Brown UNI 3/0
Body: Opal orange Estaz or hot orange pearl Tinsel Chenille
Wing: Synthetic raccoon
Collar: Brown hen neck hackle
Eyes: Mini Presentation Lead Eyes

Comments: John O'Hearn explains, "During the spring and summer months in the lower Florida Keys, some turtle grass flats may be partially covered with brown algae blooms (such as *Grassalaria*). This bonefish fly is particularly effective over such bottoms." This pattern is also known as The Gaff.

Arctic Fox Fly

Overall length: 2¼" on #4 hook
Pattern type: General attractor
Primarily designed for: Snook
Also effective on: Redfish, speckled sea trout
Submitted by: Swann's Fly Shop (Dade City, Florida)
Originated by: Various Florida guides
Tied by: Jim Swann

Hook: Mustad 34007, #2-#6
Thread: Red
Tail: Pearl Flashabou over white arctic fox tail
Eyes: Black plastic bead chain
Body: 25-lb. mono snelled, covered with red tying thread, coated with epoxy

Top view

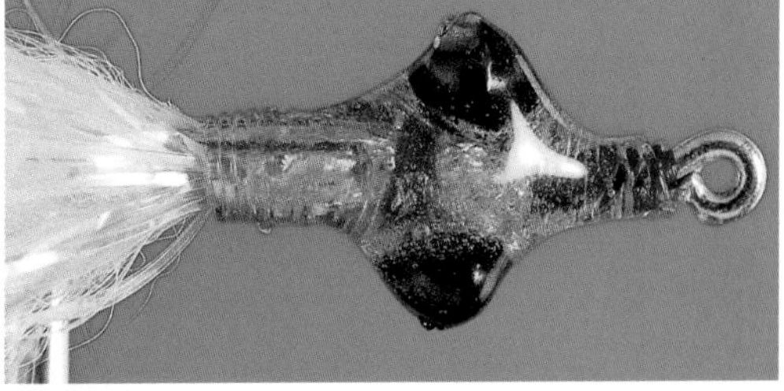

Comments: This fly was devised for fishing under lighted docks at night. It should be kept small when tying.

Arctic Shrimp

Overall length: 4" on #2 hook
Pattern type: Shrimp
Primarily designed for: Snook
Also effective on: Redfish, sea trout, bluefish, tarpon, ladyfish, jacks
Submitted by: Swann's Fly Shop (Dade City, Florida)
Originated by: Unknown
Tied by: Scott Graham

Hook: Mustad 34011, #2
Thread: Red Flat Waxed 3/0
Tail: Arctic fox tail
Eyes: Silver bead chain
Body: White/clear Ice Chenille

Comments: This pattern was designed primarily for fishing snook around lighted docks.

B.C. Crustacean

Bottom view

Overall length: 2" on #4 hook
Pattern type: Shrimp or crab
Primarily designed for: Redfish
Also effective on: Bonefish, permit, sea trout
Submitted by: The Back Country, Inc. (Vero Beach, Florida)
Originated by: Captain Eric T. Davis
Tied by: Captain Eric T. Davis

Hook: Mustad 34007, #1/0-#6
Thread: Tan
Claws: Grizzly hackle feathers flanking tan marabou with 6 strands of root beer/pearl Krystal Flash
Eyes: Black plastic beads on Dacron stalks in front; 1/8" Dazl-Eyes at rear
Body: Natural deer hair, spun and clipped
Legs: Grizzly hackle, palmered; clipped on bottom
Weed guard: Monofilament

Comments: "Work this fly," explains Captain Eric T. Davis, "over grass, and let it sit. The 'V' weed guard and lead eyes allow this fly to dart into weeds or sand, but the deer hair makes the rest of the fly sit up off the bottom, acting as a shrimp or crab does in a defensive move. The fly enters the water quietly and sinks quickly. The pattern also works well with a white body, white claws, and grizzly hackle legs."

B.C. Shrimp

Overall length: 1 3/4" on #4 hook
Pattern type: Shrimp
Primarily designed for: Bonefish, redfish
Also effective on: Permit, sea trout, sheepshead, and boxfish
Submitted by: The Back Country, Inc. (Vero Beach, Florida)
Originated by: Captain Eric T. Davis
Tied by: Captain Eric T. Davis

Hook: Mustad 34007, #2-#6; or Gamakatsu SC15, #1/0-#6
Thread: Clear Mono Thread
Claws: 2 badger hackles flanking tuft of tan marabou and 6 strands root beer Krystal Flash
Antennae: 2 strands black Ultra Hair or Supreme Hair
Legs: Badger hackle
Eyes: Black bead chain, medium or large
Body: Clear medium V-Rib over root beer/ pearl Krystal Flash
Weed guard: Monofilament

Comments: "This fly," observes Captain Eric T. Davis, "has been a great producer for a variety of species. It can be tied in many different color combinations. Tans and browns have worked the best, but try tying it in chartreuse also. The use of a 'V' weed guard make this fly an excellent choice for areas that have a lot of grass. Different weighted eyes can be used to change the sink rate."

Top view

Big Boy Tarpon Shrimp

Bottom view

Overall length: 3 1/4" on #2/0 hook
Pattern type: Grass shrimp, mantis shrimp
Primarily designed for: Tarpon
Also effective on: Snook, redfish, sea trout
Submitted by: Capt. Harry's Fishing Supply (Miami, Florida)
Originated by: Jesus Quintino
Tied by: Jesus Quintino

Hook: TMC 800S, #2/0
Thread: Fluorescent green Flat Waxed 3/0
Mouthparts: 6 strands pearl Krystal Flash over white Fly Fur
Antennae: 2 strands black Flashabou
Eyes: 60-lb. Mason nylon, melted at ends, painted black
Collar: Tan/cream rabbit strip, wrapped
Body: Large pearl Minnow Body Tubing

Big Eyed Chovy

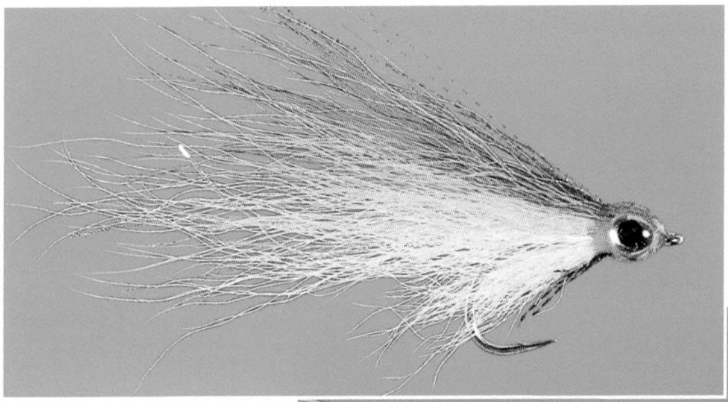

Top view

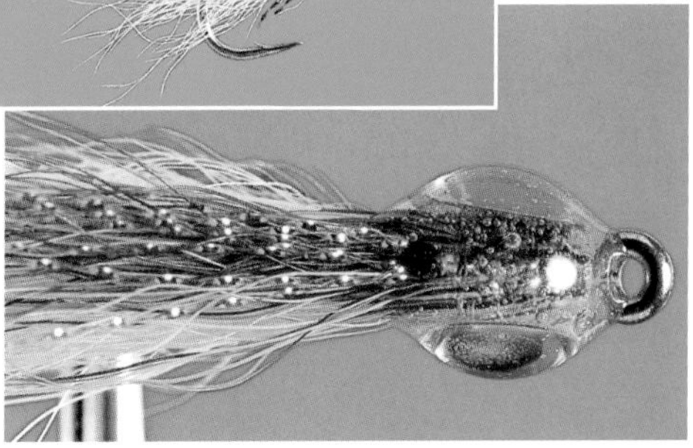

Overall length: 3" on #2 hook
Pattern type: Striped anchovy
Primarily designed for: Snook, sea trout
Also effective on: Striped bass, tarpon, jacks, ladyfish
Submitted by: The Back Country, Inc. (Vero Beach, Florida)
Originated by: Captain Eric T. Davis
Tied by: Captain Eric T. Davis

Hook: Gamakatsu SC-15, #1/0-#4
Thread: Clear Mono
Belly: White bucktail
Wing: Olive/green pearl Krystal Flash over dark fibers from yellow-dyed bucktail over yellow bucktail over Pearl Fire Fly (or substitute pearl Comes Alive) over white bucktail
Gills: Red Krystal Flash
Eyes: 3-D molded eyes coated with epoxy

Black Dog

Overall length: 4 1/2" on #1 hook
Pattern type: Baitfish
Primarily designed for: Snook, redfish, tarpon
Also effective on: Jacks, mackerel
Submitted by: Everglades Angler (Naples, Florida)
Originated by: Matt Hoover
Tied by: Matt Hoover

Hook: Mustad 34007, #3/0-#1
Thread: Black Danville Flat waxed nylon
Wing: One clump black marabou over one clump black marabou tied on each side of shank, flanked by 2 black saddle hackles one each side
Head: Tying thread
Eyes: Yellow Prism Eyes
Weed guard: Wire, tied Mullendore style

Comments: In this pattern, the feathers in the wing should be tied with concave sides together so that the feathers curve toward one another and downward. They should be 1/2" to 3/4" longer than the marabou to allow them to "swim." Epoxy around the head and eyes, but not over the eyes themselves, as the epoxy will cloud them.

Blue Crab

Comments: Captain Davis notes, "The plastic eyes on this pattern should move about freely. The heavy lead eyes make it an excellent reef fly for permit. Lighter lead eyes and a weed guard are better when fishing redfish and bonefish. With a 1/0 or 2/0 hook and heavy eyes, the fly does double duty for both permit and tarpon. This pattern doesn't need any type of flash materials.

Overall length: 2 1/4" on #1/0 hook
Pattern type: Blue crab
Primarily designed for: Permit
Also effective on: Redfish, bonefish, tarpon
Submitted by: The Back Country, Inc. (Vero Beach, Florida)
Originated by: Captain Eric T. Davis version of Jeffrey Cardenas Palmered Crab
Tied by: Captain Eric T. Davis

Hook: Mustad 34007 or Gamakatsu SC-15, #2/0-#4; weighted with lead barbell eyes behind hook eye
Thread: Brown 3/0 Monocord
Mouthparts: Natural bucktail and tan marabou
Claws: One blue grizzly hackle between two cree or variant hackles on each side
Eyes: Plastic beads on Dacron stalks
Body: Front half: cree or variant hackle, palmered; Rear half: blue grizzly and cree or variant hackle, palmered; body clipped on bottom

Bottom view

Bone Bug

Overall length: 1 1/4" on #2 hook; 1" on #4 hook
Pattern type: Crab
Primarily designed for: Bonefish, permit
Also effective on: Redfish
Submitted by: Sea Boots Outfitters (Big Pine Key, Florida)
Originated by: Captain Lenny Moffo
Tied by: Captain Lenny Moffo

Hook: Mustad 34007, or similar hook, #1/0-#8
Thread: Brown 3/0 Monocord
Body: Peacock herl (or chenille for chenille-body version)
Legs: Orange Rainy's rubber legs or Sili-Legs, or color of choice, striped with permanent marker
Eyes: Lead barbell, size according to desired sink rate
Wing: Deer hair

Top view of chenille-body version.

Comments: Captain Lenny Moffo notes, "This fly is very easy to tie, even in small sizes such as #6 or #8. The pattern also works very well in the Bahamas and Mexico."

Chip's Fat Head Minnow

Overall length: 2 1/2" on #6 hook
Pattern type: Baitfish
Primarily designed for: Redfish
Also effective on: Skipjack, perch, speckled sea trout
Submitted by: Gruene Outfitters (New Braunfels, Texas)
Originated by: Chip Evans
Tied by: Chip Evans

Hook: Mustad 34007, #4-#6
Thread: Dark brown 6/0
Weed guard: 17-lb. Mason hard mono
Tail: Brown Fly Fur over purple Lite Brite over brown Fly Fur
Body: Brown Fly Fur, spun and trimmed, colored olive on top of body and tail with permanent marker; gills colored red with permanent marker
Eyes: Spirit River 3-D Eyes, glued

Top view

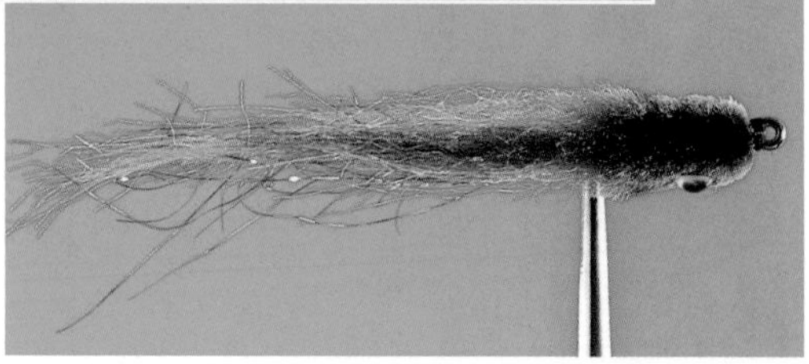

Comments: This pattern can be dressed in a variety of colors.

Chocolate Eel

Overall length: 2 1/4" on #6 hook
Pattern type: Small eel
Primarily designed for: Redfish
Also effective on: Sea trout, black drum
Submitted by: Padre Outfitters (South Padre Island, Texas)
Originated by: Captain Eric Glass
Tied by: Captain Eric Glass

Hook: TMC 811S, #4-#6
Thread: Tan Danville Plus
Weed guard: 15-lb. Mason hard monofilament
Wing: Dark grayish brown ostrich herl over sparse bunch of orange Flashabou dubbing mixed with a few strands of copper Flashabou over light brown bucktail
Eyes: Copper or gold bead chain, extra small
Head: Black/tan variegated chenille, medium

Comments: Though a staunch advocate of catch-and-release, Captain Glass says that he'll always jump at the chance to examine carcasses around the fish-cleaning table, and this fly may imitate small eels that show up among the stomach contents. He explains, "This is an excellent all-around fly for sight-fishing redfish. We use it mostly over dark or grassy bottoms. It's useful for less-than-aggressive cruising reds, since it's a drab, unobtrusive fly. I usually ease it along at a slower pace than I would a large or bright attractor. It may imitate a small eel, dark goby, or other small fish."

Cole's Peel & Eat Shrimp

Overall length: Body 1 3/4", antennae 2 1/2", on #2 hook
Pattern type: Shrimp
Primarily designed for: Redfish and bonefish
Also effective on: Snook
Submitted by: Boca Grande Outfitters (Boca Grande, Florida)
Originated by: Cole Fairbanks
Tied by: Cole Fairbanks

Hook: Mustad 34011, #2
Thread: Tan Monocord
Weed guard: Monofilament line
Antennae: Stripped grizzly hackle stems
Eyes: Monofilament
Body: Pearl Estaz
Legs: Ginger grizzly hackle palmered over Estaz body
Shellback: Swiss Straw
Tail: Swiss Straw from shellback

Top view

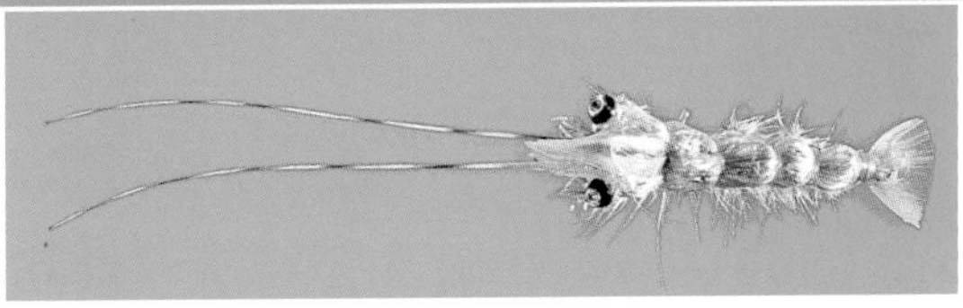

Comments: To tie this fly, mount mono for weed guard and the eyes at rear of hook. Mount body material, hackle, and Swiss Straw between eyes. Wrap body material to hook eye, followed by hackle. Return tying thread to hook bend by spiraling over body. Pull shellback to hook eye and created segmentations with tying thread. Attach free end of weed guard behind eye. Trim tail to shape. Cover shellback with light coat of Dave's Flexament.

Cowen's Coyote

Overall length: 3 1/4" on #1 hook
Pattern type: General attractor
Primarily designed for: Striped bass
Also effective on: False albacore, bonito, bluefish, weakfish, redfish, sea trout (southern), barracuda, snook, tarpon,
Submitted by: The Fish Hawk (Atlanta, Georgia)
Originated by: Henry Cowen and Blakemore Roadrunner
Tied by: Henry Cowen

Hook: TMC 811S or Eagle Claw 254SS, #2/0-#4
Thread: Danville monofilament, fine
Wing: Olive bucktail (chartreuse for chartreuse version)
Belly: White rabbit Zonker strip with mono spike post (see comment)
Eyes: 5/32" black weighted Real Eyes with 1.5 Prismatic Stick-on eyes
Spinner assembly: Size 12 barrel swivel; size 0 split ring; size 00 Colorado spinner blade

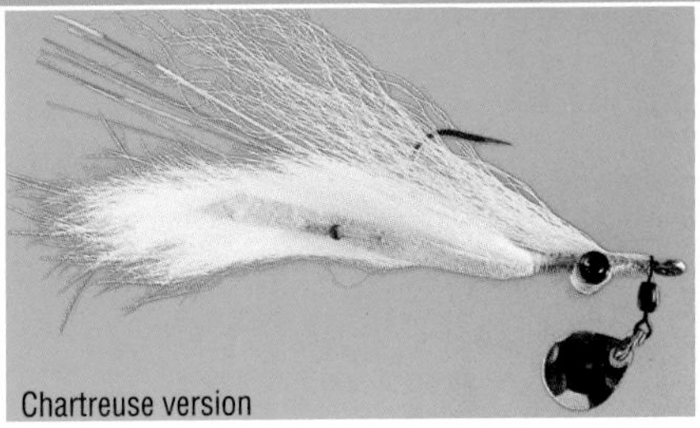

Chartreuse version

Comments: The mono spike used in the tail is a 30-lb. clear monofilament that prevents the tail from fouling. To form the tail, mount the mono atop the shank behind the eyes so that it projects about 2" past hook bend. Mount rabbit strip with the fur side against the hook shank. Pierce a hole in the rabbit strip about 1/2" past hook bend. Thread mono through hole from the fur side; when fly is complete melt a ball on the end of the mono (visible as a small dark ball in the photos).

To form spinner assembly, slide swivel over hook point. Dress the fly. Use thread wraps at head to position the swivel opposite the hook point, on the same side of the shank as the eyes. Attach split ring and spinner. Indiana style or willow leaf blades can also be used.

Designer Henry Cowen says this is an excellent searching pattern. Along with this fly, he included a letter from the International Game Fish Association (IGFA), which determined that, despite the spinner here, this pattern is regarded as a fly and any fish taken with it and submitted for world-record status would be considered a fly-caught fish.

Cowen's E-Z Body Baitfish

Overall length: 3 1/2" on #1 hook
Pattern type: Thin-bodied baitfish: shad, silversides, sand eel
Primarily designed for: Striped bass, false albacore
Also effective on: Bluefish, redfish, bonito, weakfish, snook, sea trout (southern)
Submitted by: The Fish Hawk (Atlanta, Georgia)
Originated by: Inspired by Bob Popovic's Rabbit Candy
Tied by: Henry Cowen

Hook: TMC 811S or Eagle Claw 254SS, #2/0-#4
Thread: Danville monofilament, fine
Tail: White rabbit Zonker strip with mono spike post (see comment)
Wings: Peacock herl over white fly fur (chartreuse fur for chartreuse version) over Pearl Flashabou
Body: E-Z Body Braid (medium) slipped over front of fly and secured behind eye; completely coated (lightly) with epoxy
Eyes: 1.5 silver Prismatic Stick-on eyes

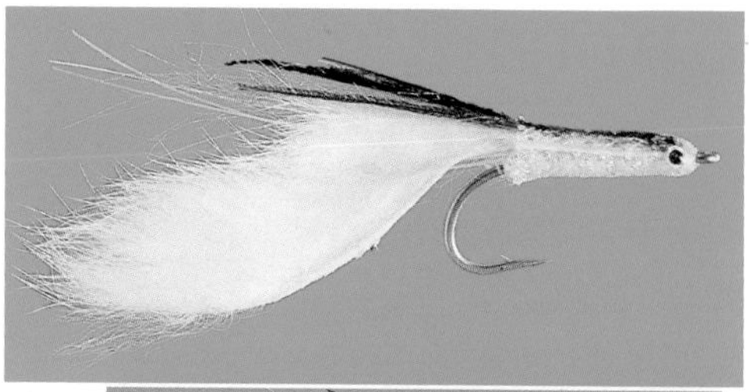

Chartreuse version

Comments: The mono spike used in the tail is a 30-lb. clear monofilament that prevents the tail from fouling. To form the tail, mount the mono atop the shank so that it projects about 2" past hook bend. Mount rabbit strip with the hide side against the hook shank. Pierce a hole in the rabbit strip about 1/2" past hook bend. Thread mono through hole from the hide side; when fly is complete melt a ball on the end of the mono (visible as a small dark ball in the photos).

Cowen's Magnum Bunker

Overall length: 7" on #4/0 hook
Pattern type: Moss bunker or menhaden
Primarily designed for: Striped bass
Also effective on: Redfish, bluefish, weakfish, tarpon, barracuda, snook, cobia
Submitted by: The Fish Hawk (Atlanta, Georgia)
Originated by: Henry Cowen
Tied by: Henry Cowen

Hook: TMC 800S or Eagle Claw 254SS, #4/0; weighted with .030" or .035" lead wire
Thread: Danville monofilament, fine
Tail: White bucktail, long and stiff fibers
Body: Pearl Sparkle Braid
Wing: Peacock herl over dark olive Icelandic sheep hair over light olive Icelandic sheep hair over Pearl Flashabou over white Icelandic sheep hair; black spot added with waterproof marker
Belly: White Icelandic sheep hair
Gills: Red Krystal Flash
Lateral line: Pearl Flashabou
Eyes: 7/16" Prismatic Epoxy Eyes (gold)

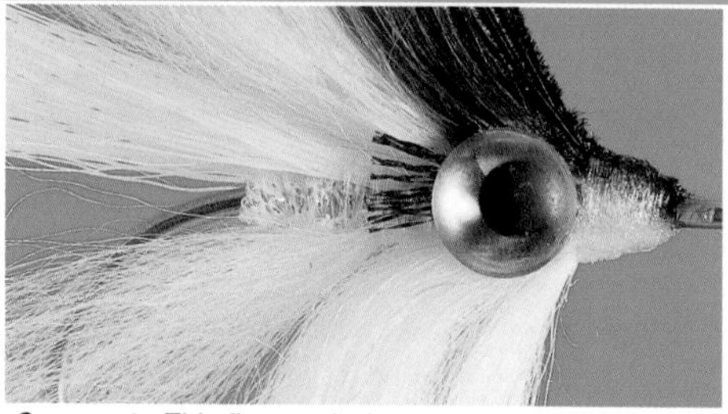

Detail of staggered mount for wing and belly hair

Comments: This fly was designed to catch stripers in the Northeast from Cape Cod to Sandy Hook, New Jersey. Henry Cowen notes that the fly is light for its size and can easily be cast with a 9-weight rod.

Cowen's Magnum Herring

Overall length: 6 1/2" on #4/0 hook
Pattern type: Atlantic blueback herring
Primarily designed for: Striped bass
Also effective on: Bluefish, false albacore, barracuda, cobia
Submitted by: The Fish Hawk (Atlanta, Georgia)
Originated by: Henry Cowen
Tied by: Henry Cowen

Hook: TMC 800S or Eagle Claw 254SS, #4/0; weighted with .030" or .035" lead wire
Thread: Danville monofilament, fine
Tail: White bucktail, long and stiff fibers
Body: Pearl Sparkle Braid
Wing: Peacock herl over blue Icelandic sheep hair over white Icelandic sheep hair over Pearl Flashabou over white Icelandic sheep hair
Belly: White Icelandic sheep hair
Gills: Red Krystal Flash
Lateral line: Pink Holographic Flash
Eyes: 7/16" Prismatic Epoxy Eyes (silver)

Comments: This fly was designed for late-season striper fishing (October to December) when the herring make their annual run from Cape Cod to Sandy Hook, New Jersey. It is particularly effective at Montauk Point and in Long Island Sound. The belly and wing hair are tied in bunches staggered along the hook shank as shown in the supplementary photo under Cowen's Magnum Bunker, above.

Cowen's Swimming Mini-Menhaden

Overall length: 3 1/4" on #1/0 hook
Pattern type: Baby bunker, mini-menhaden
Primarily designed for: Striped bass
Also effective on: Bluefish, bonito, false albacore, weakfish, redfish, sea trout (southern), snook, cobia
Submitted by: The Fish Hawk (Atlanta, Georgia)
Originated by: Inspired by Eric Peterson design
Tied by: Henry Cowen

Hook: TMC 811S, #3/0-#2; weighted with .030" or .035" lead wire
Thread: Danville monofilament, fine
Tail: White saltwater marabou
Body: Pearl Sparkle Braid
Collar: White bucktail
Wings: 4 strands peacock herl over olive bucktail over lavender bucktail over Pearl Flashabou
Throat: Red Krystal Flash
Eyes: 1.5 Prismatic Stick-on eyes (gold)

Comments: Originator Henry Cowen explains that this pattern imitates any "wide profile" baitfish and has a breathing/swimming action underwater. He also ties a chartreuse and white version.

Crab

Overall length: 1 1/2" on #2 hook
Pattern type: Crab
Primarily designed for: Redfish
Also effective on: Bonefish, permit
Submitted by: Swann's Fly Shop (Dade City, Florida)
Originated by: Jim Swann
Tied by: Jim Swann

Hook: Mustad 34007, #2-#6
Thread: Brown
Tail: 2 yellow grizzly neck hackles
Underbody: Yellow grizzly hackle palmered over brown Ice Chenille
Eyes: Lead barbell painted white with black pupils
Shellback: Brown Furry Foam, lightly coated with epoxy

Bottom view

Comments: Tyer Jim Swann also recommends dressing this pattern with a double monofilament weed guard.

Cypert's Minnow

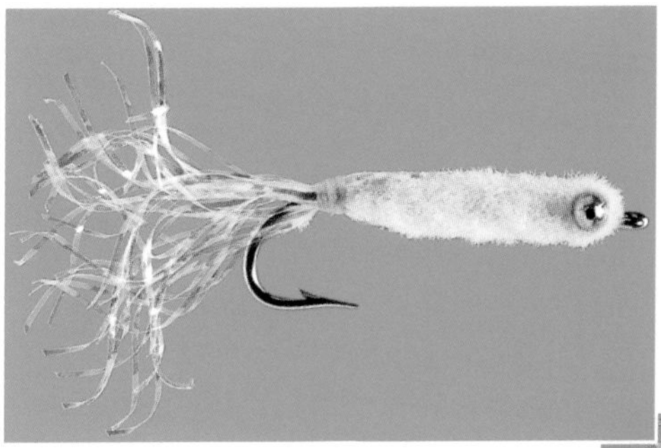

Overall length: 2" on #4 hook
Pattern type: Baitfish
Primarily designed for: Redfish
Also effective on: Speckled trout, striped bass, and most predatory species
Submitted by: Cypert's Waterbugs, Inc. (Aquilla, Texas)
Originated by: Charlie Cypert
Tied by: Charlie Cypert

Hook: Mustad 34011, #2-#6
Thread: Chartreuse Flat waxed nylon (black for green-bodied version)
Tail: Pearl Mylar cord from belly/dorsal stripe, unraveled
Body: Chartreuse chenille (green Krystal Flash for green-bodied version)
Eyes: Silver bead chain (or dumbbell eyes)
Belly/dorsal Stripe: Pearl Mylar cord

Comments: Charlie Cypert explains, "On the Gulf flats in Texas, there are times when the redfish reject all the standard favorites, but will eat this fly. It has saved the day several times for Freddy Lynch (mid-Texas coast guide), myself, and friends. The best color for redfish is pearl/chartreuse. A red body with gold flash also works well."

To tie the belly/dorsal strip, poke a hole in the center of the Mylar cord and insert the hook eye into the hole. Pull one end of the cord tight over the top of the fly, the other end along the belly. Bind down and rear of body and fray to form tail.

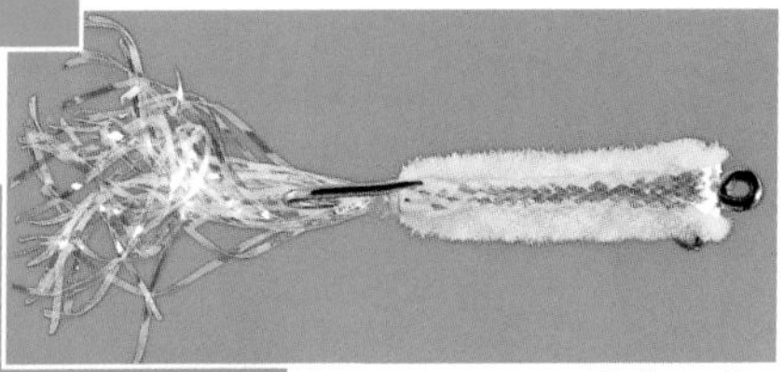

Bottom view

Version with green body

Cypert's Scissor Tail

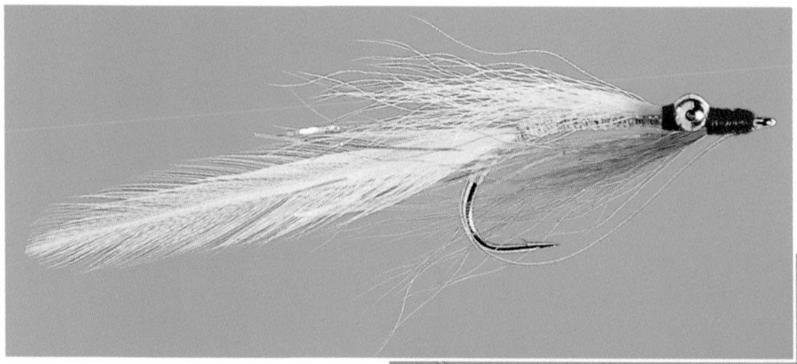

Top view

Overall length: 3 1/2" on #1/0 hook
Pattern type: Baitfish
Primarily designed for: Striped bass, redfish, speckled trout
Submitted by: Cypert's Waterbugs, Inc. (Aquilla, Texas)
Originated by: Charlie Cypert
Tied by: Charlie Cypert

Hook: Mustad 34011SS or equivalent, #4/0-#4
Thread: Red Flat waxed nylon
Weed guard: Monofilament, loop style
Tail: 2 white saltwater/bass saddle or neck hackles
Body: Pearl Flashabou
Wing: White Bucktail
Eyes: Silver bead chain
Throat: Blue/gray bucktail over pearl Flashabou

Comments: Charlie Cypert explains, "This fly was designed for stripers in clear water when they would reject a bulkier pattern. It gives the silhouette of a baitfish when tied very sparse. The saddle hackle tail adds extra movement when the fly is fished slow, with quick strips and a pause to allow it to suspend and sink like a dying baitfish. We found out that it works well on redfish and speckled trout on the Gulf coast and bass on inland lakes. We change the color and size to fit the type of fish."

Cypert's Slim Jim

Overall length: 3 1/4" on #4 hook
Pattern type: Baitfish
Primarily designed for: Speckled trout
Also effective on: Redfish, striped bass
Submitted by: Cypert's Waterbugs, Inc. (Aquilla, Texas)
Originated by: Charlie Cypert
Tied by: Charlie Cypert

Hook: 3XL or 4XL, #1/0-#6
Thread: White Flat waxed nylon
Tail: Pearl Flashabou over blue/gray bucktail over white bucktail (or saddle hackle)
Body: Pearl Flashabou
Head: Gold bead (or bead chain or conehead)

Comments: "This sparse fly," says Charlie Cypert, "is productive in clear water when the fish ignore bulkier patterns. It can be fished slow, with pauses, or very fast for reaction strikes. We tie it in sizes and colors to match various species of fish."

Deer Hair Saltwater Diver

Top view

Overall length: 2 1/2" on #6 hook
Pattern type: General attractor
Effective on: Snook, redfish, speckled sea trout
Submitted by: Swann's Fly Shop (Dade City, Florida)
Originated by: Adaptation of Larry Dahlberg pattern
Tied by: Jim Swann

Hook: TMC 8089NP, #6
Thread: Black
Weed guard: Double strand monofilament
Tail: Pearl Flashabou over white marabou flanked by one badger or variant saddle hackle on each side
Collar: Clipped natural deer hair over natural deer hair tips
Body: White, black, and brown deer hair, stacked and clipped as shown

Don's Popping Shrimp

Comments: On this pattern, epoxy holds all materials to the popper body, and the body itself to the hook shank.

Bottom view

Overall length: 4 1/4" on #2 hook
Pattern type: Shrimp
Primarily designed for: Speckled trout
Also effective on: Redfish
Submitted by: Shrevetown Fly Shop (Shreveport, Louisiana)
Originated by: Don Lawler
Tied by: Don Lawler

Hook: TMC 511S, #2
Thread: 3/0
Tail: Brown Super Hair
Body: Size #2 popper body, coated with epoxy
Legs: Tan Cactus Chenille
Eyes: Doll eyes painted with black nail polish
Antennae: White Flashabou

DT

Overall length: 3" on #1 hook
Pattern type: General attractor
Primarily designed for: Snook on beaches
Also effective on: Jacks
Submitted by: Everglades Angler (Naples, Florida)
Originated by: Duane White version of Stu Apte design
Tied by: Duane White

Hook: Mustad 34007, #1-#2
Thread: White Flat waxed nylon
Wing: Pearl Krystal Flash mixed with white FisHair over 2 white neck hackles over Pearl Krystal Flash mixed white FisHair
Hackle: White neck hackles

Epoxy Charlie

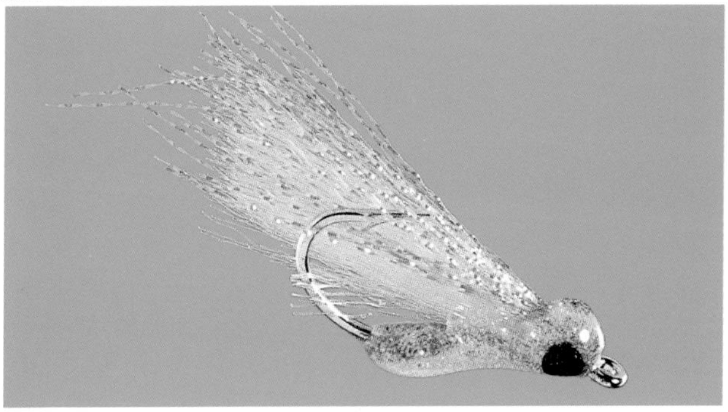

Overall length: 1 1/2" on #4 hook
Pattern type: General attractor, shrimp
Primarily designed for: Bonefish
Also effective on: Snook, redfish, speckled sea trout
Submitted by: Swann's Fly Shop (Dade City, Florida)
Originated by: Unknown
Tied by: Jim Swann

Hook: Mustad 34007, #2-#8
Thread: Chartreuse
Wing: Pearl Krystal Flash over white FisHair
Body: Chartreuse glitter epoxy over snelled monofilament underbody
Eyes: Painted black under epoxy

Epoxy Minnow

Top view

Overall length: 2 1/4" on #4 hook
Pattern type: Glass minnow
Primarily designed for: All saltwater species
Submitted by: Swann's Fly Shop (Dade City, Florida)
Originated by: Carl Hansen
Tied by: Jim Swann

Hook: Mustad 34007, #2-#8
Thread: Pink
Tail: White FisHair surrounded by pearl Polar Flash
Body: 25-lb. monofilament snelled Carl Hanson style, coated with epoxy
Gills: Painted under epoxy
Eyes: Painted under epoxy

Epoxy Minnow

Overall length: 3″ on #2 hook
Pattern type: Glass minnow
Primarily designed for: Redfish
Also effective on: Sea trout, jacks, snook, small tarpon, ladyfish
Submitted by: Fly Shop of Fort Lauderdale (Fort Lauderdale, Florida)
Originated by: Ed Norton
Tied by: Ed Norton

Hook: Mustad 34011, #2
Thread: Clear nylon
Tail: Olive bucktail over white bucktail, secured behind hook eye
Dorsal line: Green Mylar braid
Ventral line: White Mylar braid
Body: Epoxy
Eyes: Painted, yellow with black pupils

Top view

Comments: Ed Norton explains, "I fish this fly when fish are busting up glass minnows at Flamingo (Everglades National Park). It can be tied in any color.

Epoxy Slider

Overall length: 1 1/2″ on #4 hook
Pattern type: Shrimp
Primarily designed for: Bonefish
Also effective on: Sea trout, redfish
Submitted by: Fly Shop of Fort Lauderdale (Fort Lauderdale, Florida)
Originated by: Ed Norton
Tied by: Ed Norton

Hook: Mustad 3407, #4
Thread: Tan
Antennae & mouthparts: Tan marabou and frayed pearlescent tubing from body
Eyes: Black lead barbell eyes
Body: Pearlescent Mylar tubing attached behind hook eye, pulled around outside of each barbell eyes, coated with epoxy

Top view

Comments: Ed Norton notes, "This fly is good for tailing fish and fish swimming with stingrays. Because of its shape, you can throw past the fish and strip the fly fast; when you stop it, the fly flutters to the bottom and rides with the hook point up."

Flats Burger

Overall length: 1″ on #4 hook
Pattern type: Crab
Primarily designed for: Redfish
Also effective on: Sheepshead
Submitted by: Padre Outfitters (South Padre Island, Texas)
Originated by: Bill Hagen
Tied by: Bill Hagen

Hook: Mustad 34007, #4
Thread: White Flymaster Plus
Mouthparts: Grizzly marabou
Body: Bleached deer hair, spun and clipped
Legs: Black round rubber
Eyes: Black glass beads glued on 22-lb. monofilament, which is then burned at the ends to create pupils

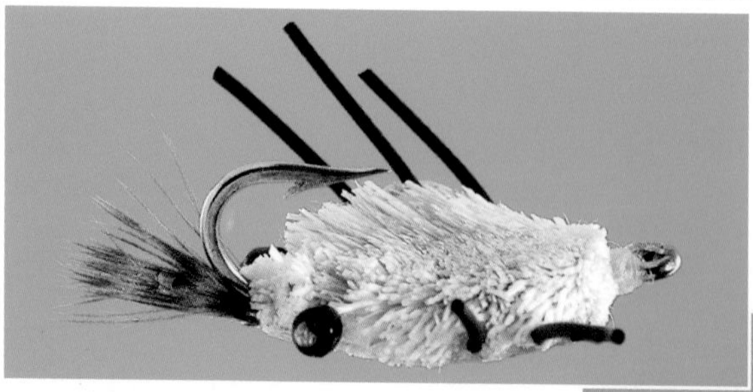

Bottom view

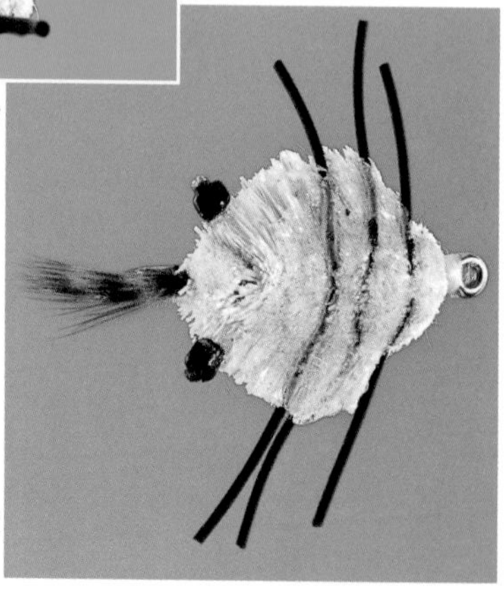

Comments: Bill Hagen notes, "This pattern imitates any of the variety of mud crabs that spend time on the water's surface. It's a very fun pattern to fish, although the water must be reasonably clear. Many times fish will rise to this fly slowly and take a long look before they eat. The fly should be manipulated so it barely moves if the fish hesitates to strike. It's an effective pattern throughout the day, and fish don't mind rising from 2 or 3 feet of water to eat the fly, even with bright skies. (I know it's ugly)."

To tie the legs, work 3 or 4 pieces of round rubber into the hair, and coat with Stick 'N Seal adhesive, which you spread with moist fingers. After forming the eyes, coat the mono shafts with Stick 'N Seal and insert them into the crab body. They will hold firmly.

Fleeing Crab

Overall length: 2" on #4 hook
Pattern type: Fleeing crab
Primarily designed for: Permit, bonefish
Also effective on: Redfish
Submitted by: Sea Boots Outfitters (Big Pine Key, Florida)
Originated by: Captain Lenny Moffo
Tied by: Captain Lenny Moffo

Hook: Mustad 34007, #1-#8
Thread: Chartreuse Danville 3/0 Flat-waxed, or color to match body
Legs: Light tan Rainy's rubber or Sili-Legs, striped with permanent brown marker
Underbody: Chartreuse tying thread (brown thread for brown version)
Body: Alternating bands of tan and brown Aunt Lydia's yarn (cream and tan yarn for brown version)
Eyes: Wapsi lead barbell, size according to desired sink rate
Weed guard (optional): 10-lb. Maxima Chameleon, striped with permanent marker

Top view of brown version at top; green version at bottom.

FuzBone

Overall length: 1 1/4" on #6 hook
Pattern type: Shrimp, crab
Primarily designed for: Bonefish
Also effective on: Pompano, permit, sheepshead, redfish
Submitted by: The Back Country, Inc. (Vero Beach, Florida)
Originated by: Paul Ringold
Tied by: Paul Ringold

Hook: Mustad 34007, #4-#8
Thread: 2-lb. Ande clear monofilament
Body: Pearl Flashabou coated with head cement
Head: Pinch leech yarn
Eyes: Black medium bead chain
Wing: Tan grizzly hackle tips, splayed
Hackle: Grizzly hackle palmered in front of eyes

Top view

Comments: This pattern is also effective tied in tan, olive, and black.

Giant Dahlberg

Overall length: 6" on #4/0 hook
Pattern type: General attractor
Primarily designed for: Snook
Also effective on: Tied in appropriate sizes, just about anything
Submitted by: The Back Country, Inc. (Vero Beach, Florida)
Originated by: Larry Dahlberg
Tied by: Captain Eric T. Davis

Hook: Mustad 34007, #4/0-#1
Thread: Chartreuse Flymaster Plus
Tail: Silver Krystal Flash over chartreuse yak hair flanked by pearl Flashabou and pearl Krystal Flash
Collar: Chartreuse marabou
Gills: Red marabou
Head: Chartreuse deer belly hair, spun and clipped, coated with Softex
Eyes: Doll eyes glued to head

Comments: "I add Softex to the base of the yak hair tail," explains Captain Davis. "It keeps the hair from fouling around the hook. Softex also works great on the deer hair. It makes the fibers very durable and stiff, and the fly will float all day long. This fly needs at least a 10-weight rod to throw it, but around docks and bridges at night, watch out. It has a big profile for big fish."

Front view

Glass Bead Shrimp

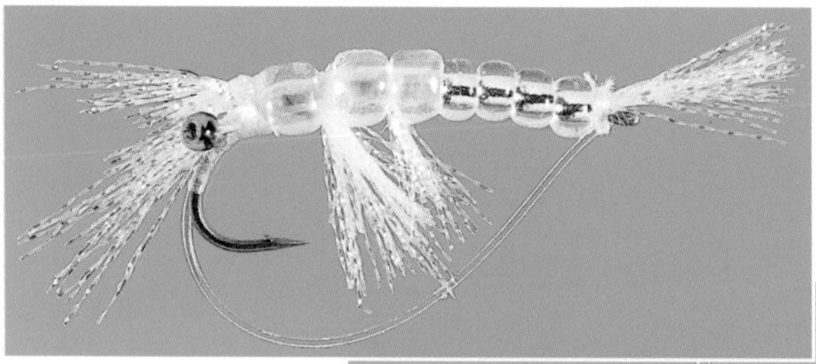

Pink version

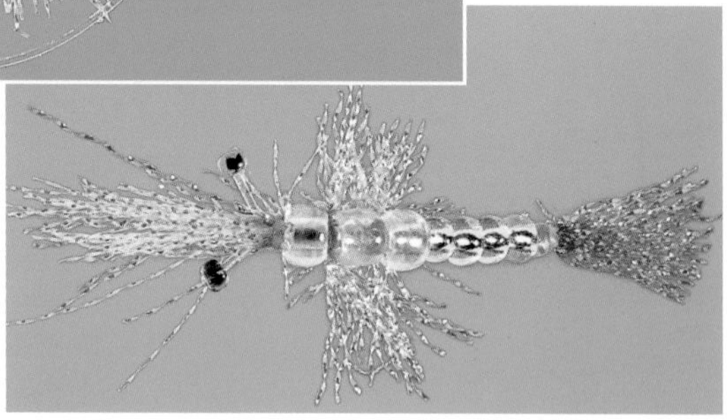

Overall length: 2 1/4" on #2 hook
Pattern type: Grass shrimp
Primarily designed for: Redfish, sea trout
Also effective on: Black drum
Submitted by: Brazos Fly Fishers (Granbury, Texas)
Originated by: Richard Hart
Tied by: Richard Hart

Hook: Partridge CS54 shrimp, #2
Thread: White Danville Flat waxed nylon
Weed guard: 12-lb. Mason hard nylon
Antennae & mouthparts: Pearl Krystal Flash (pink for pink version)
Eyes: Jalapeno colored Killer Caddis beads glued to 30-lb. Mason nylon
Body: 4 large and 3 extra-large pearl Killer Caddis beads
Legs: Pearl Krystal Flash (pink for pink version)
Tail: Pearl Krystal Flash (pink for pink version)

Comments: Tyer Richard Hart notes, "I'd rather be fishing! My patterns are simple and quick, less time at the bench and more on the water. Synthetic materials are strong and hold up to toothy fish."

Glass Minnow, Bullethead

Top view

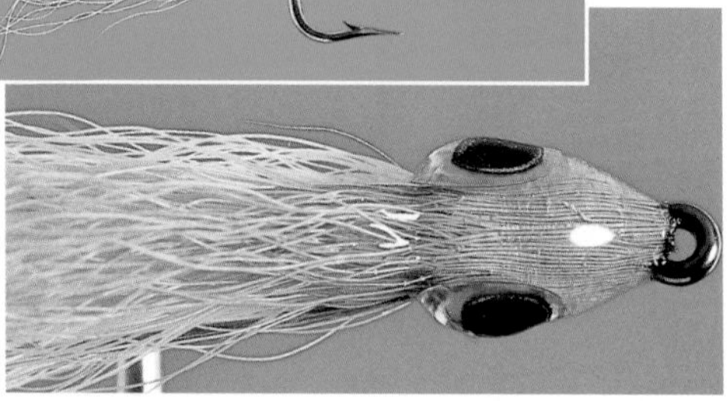

Overall length: 3 1/4" on #2 hook
Pattern type: Glass minnow
Primarily designed for: All saltwater species
Submitted by: The Back Country, Inc. (Vero Beach, Florida)
Originated by: Adapted from a variety of glass minnow patterns
Tied by: John Fuchs

Hook: Mustad 34007, #2
Thread: Mono
Body: Clear V-Rib, size small, over silver Mylar tinsel underbody
Wing: Blue bucktail over lime green bucktail over gray aqua bucktail flanked by silver holographic Fly Fiber
Eyes: 6mm holographic eyes, silver with black pupils
Head: 30-minute epoxy, bullet shaped

Glass Spoon Fly

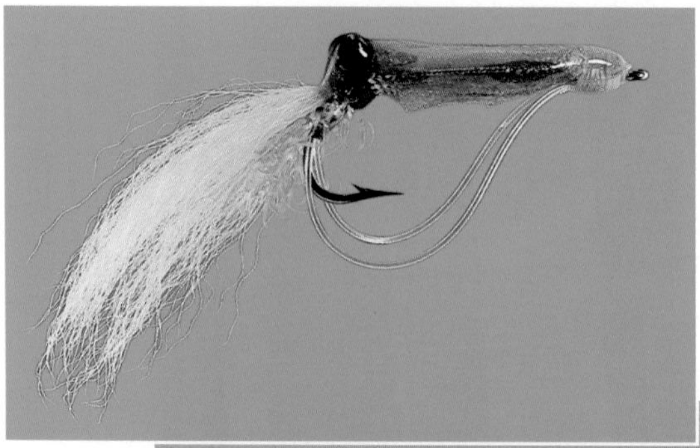

Top view

Overall length: 2 1/2" on #4 hook
Pattern type: General attractor
Effective on: All saltwater species, particularly snook, redfish, speckled trout
Submitted by: Swann's Fly Shop (Dade City, Florida)
Originated by: Jim Swann
Tied by: Jim Swann

Hook: Mustad 34011, #4
Thread: Chartreuse
Weed guard: Double strand monofilament
Tail: Chartreuse calf tail over frayed ends of body tubing
Eyes: Black plastic bead chain, coated with epoxy
Underbody: Hard plastic trimmed to shape
Overbody: Chartreuse Mylar tubing sleeved over underbody, coated with epoxy

Gold Spoon

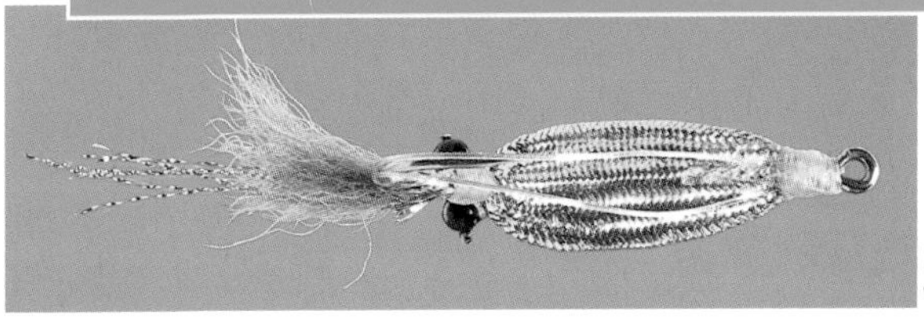

Bottom view

Overall length: 3" on #1/0 hook
Pattern type: General attractor
Primarily designed for: Redfish
Also effective on: Snook, speckled sea trout
Submitted by: Swann's Fly Shop (Dade City, Florida)
Originated by: Unknown
Tied by: Jim Swann

Hook: Mustad 34011, #1/0-#6
Thread: Yellow
Weed guard: Double strand of monofilament
Tail: Orange calf tail over gold Krystal Flash
Eyes: Black plastic bead chain
Underbody: Hard plastic, cut to shape
Body: Gold Mylar tubing sleeved over underbody; tubing and eyes coated lightly with epoxy

Graham's Deceiver (Tan/White/Grizzly)

Overall length: 3 1/2" on #1/0 hook
Pattern type: White bait, greenbacks, scaled sardines
Primarily designed for: Snook, sea trout, redfish
Also effective on: Jacks, small tarpon, ladyfish, bluefish
Submitted by: Swann's Fly Shop (Dade City, Florida)
Originated by: Lefty Kreh
Tied by: Scott Graham

Hook: Mustad 77660SS, #1/0
Thread: White Flat Waxed 3/0
Tail: Pearl Flashabou mixed
Wing: Peacock herl over green/silver holographic Flashabou over 8 gray saddle hackles flanked by one brown grizzly hackle feather on each side
Belly: White arctic fox fur
Eyes: Red holographic Stick-on eyes

Graham's Finger Mullet Magnum

Overall length: 3 1/2" on #1/0 hook
Pattern type: Mullet
Primarily designed for: Snook, sea trout
Also effective on: Redfish, ladyfish, bluefish
Submitted by: Swann's Fly Shop (Dade City, Florida)
Originated by: Unknown
Tied by: Scott Graham

Hook: Mustad 77660SS, #1/0
Thread: Red Flat Waxed 3/0
Wing: Copper Krystal Flash over 2 grizzly saddles hackles on each side
Gills: Red deer hair
Head: Chartreuse deer body hair stacked over white deer body hair, clipped to shape
Eyes: Red holographic Stick-on eyes, glued on

Graham's Mullet (Brown Phase)

Overall length: 3" on #1/0 hook
Pattern type: Finger mullet, mud minnow
Primarily designed for: Redfish, snook
Also effective on: Sea trout, ladyfish, small tarpon
Submitted by: Swann's Fly Shop (Dade City, Florida)
Originated by: Unknown
Tied by: Scott Graham

Hook: Mustad 77660SS, #1/0
Thread: Red Flat Waxed 3/0
Wing: Copper Krystal Flash over 2 brown grizzly hackles on each side
Gills: Red deer hair
Head: Natural brown deer body hair stacked over white deer body hair, clipped to shape
Eyes: Red holographic Stick-on eyes, glued on

Greg's Blonde

Overall length: 2 1/2" on #2 hook
Pattern type: Baitfish
Primarily designed for: General saltwater use
Submitted by: Greg Miheve, Master Fly Tier (Ft. Walton Beach, Florida)
Originated by: Greg Miheve version of Joe Brooks design
Tied by: Greg Miheve

Hook: Mustad 34007 or TMC 811S, #3/0-#6
Thread: Fluorescent fire orange Flat waxed nylon
Tail: 6-8 strands pearl Krystal Flash over white bucktail flanked by 6-8 strands pearl Flashabou on each side
Body: Pearl Flashabou wrapped in double layer over tying thread base, lacquered
Wing: Peacock Krystal Flash over pearl Krystal Flash over white bucktail flanked by pearl Flashabou
Eyes: Painted, yellow with black pupils

Comments: Greg Miheve notes, "The addition of a fire orange head and peacock Krystal Flash seems to have really improved on Joe Brooks' Platinum Blonde."

Greg's Bottom Feeder

Bottom view

Overall length: 2 1/2" on #4 hook
Pattern type: Baitfish
Primarily designed for: Redfish, sea trout
Also effective on: Bonefish, bluefish, jacks
Submitted by: Greg Miheve, Master Fly Tier (Ft. Walton Beach, Florida)
Originated by: Greg Miheve
Tied by: Greg Miheve

Hook: Mustad 34011 or TMC 9394, #2/0- #4; shank bent 45-degrees toward hook point 1/4" behind eye
Thread: White Flat waxed nylon (orange for brown/orange version)
Tail: White bucktail flanked by 4-5 strands silver (or pearl) Flashabou on each side (orange bucktail and gold Flashabou for brown/orange version)
Body: Silver Mylar tinsel (gold tinsel for brown/orange version)
Eyes: Nickel-plated brass barbell eyes, attached with red thread, pupils painted black (gold eyes for brown/orange version); head and eyes coated with epoxy
Wing: Lime green bucktail over white bucktail flanked by 4-6 strands lime green Flashabou on each side (brown bucktail over orange bucktail flanked by gold Flashabou for brown/orange version)

Brown/orange version

Comments: "Unlike a Clouser, which lies flat," notes Greg Miheve, "this fly 'stands on its head' as does a bottom-feeding baitfish, digging up a puff of sand or mud, which attracts everything from flounders to stripers. Exceptionally good fly for redfish."

Greg's Cobia Pulsar

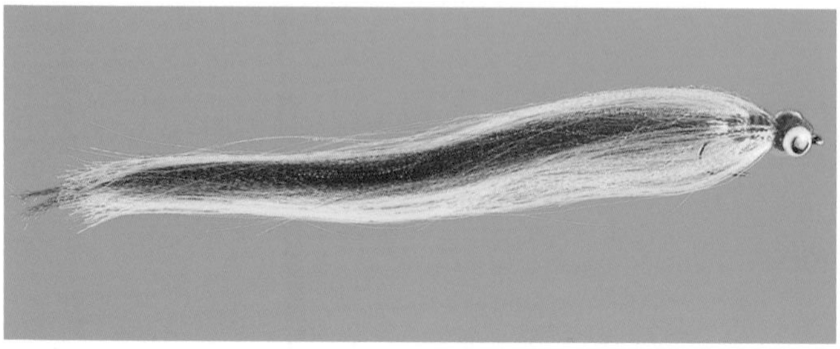

Overall length: 10 3/4" on #4/0 hook
Pattern type: Squid, eel
Primarily designed for: Cobia
Also effective on: Amberjack, king mackerel, other large fish found near offshore oil rigs
Submitted by: Greg Miheve, Master Fly Tier (Ft. Walton Beach, Florida)
Originated by: Greg Miheve
Tied by: Greg Miheve

Hook: Mustad 3407SS or TMC 800S, #6/0-#2/0
Thread: Fluorescent orange Flat waxed nylon
Tail: Thick hank of fluorescent orange Ultra Hair, 15-25 strands each orange Krystal Flash and orange Flashabou distributed around Ultra Hair
Body: 2 bumps formed of fluorescent orange chenille; tied in front of each bump to surround it are a sparse amount of chartreuse Ultra Hair and 20-30 strands each chartreuse Krystal Flash and chartreuse Flashabou

Head: Fluorescent orange chenille
Eyes: Extra-large lead eyes, filed flat on ends; 10mm doll eyes, yellow with black pupils, glued to ends of lead eyes; head and eyes coated with epoxy

Detail of body construction.

Comments: Greg Miheve says, "A spectacularly successful cobia fly—also great for offshore oil rig monsters (jacks, mackerel, sharks, grouper). Other good colors are pink over red, purple/red, chartreuse, white/ fluorescent pink, olive/chartreuse."

Greg's Flats Fly

Top view

Other versions clockwise from upper left: banded-gray; white LiveHart version; orange butt amber; chartreuse

Overall length: 1 1/2" on #4 hook
Pattern type: Small crustacean
Primarily designed for: Bonefish, permit
Also effective on: Redfish, speckled sea trout, striped bass, croaker, surf perch (West Coast)
Submitted by: Greg Miheve, Master Fly Tier (Ft. Walton Beach, Florida)
Originated by: Greg Miheve
Tied by: Greg Miheve

Hook: Mustad 34007 or TMC 800S, #4-#8
Thread: White Danville Flat waxed nylon
Tail: Light tan calf tail, body length, split 90 degrees, flanked with 2-3 strands root beer Krystal Flash on each side
Body: Pearl Flashabou overwrapped with 4 bands of tan tying thread, then whole body overwrapped with clear V-Rib
Hackle: Ginger grizzly with the left side (viewed from the front) stripped off, mounted by tip and palmered; try to get at least 6 wraps; clipped on bottom
Eyes: Bead chain (or substitute metal barbell or lead eyes)
Weed guard (optional): 20-lb. Mason hard mono
Head: Tan Danville Flat waxed nylon (or other colors as pictured in supplementary photo)

Side view of banded-tan version with chartreuse head and weed guard.

Comments: Greg Miheve notes that this pattern has been the top permit fly at Casa Blanca for the past 2 years and is especially good for big bonefish in the Florida Keys. The LiveHart version (pictured in supplementary photo) has a band of red thread under the V-Rib just behind the eyes to simulate the internal organs often seen in translucent crustaceans such as shrimp. This version is productive in cream, yellow, and chartreuse, as well as white. Miheve uses white thread on all patterns to highlight the Flashabou underbody; the head is finished in various colors as pictured.

Greg's Redfish Furtail

Overall length: 3 3/4" on #2 hook
Pattern type: Sculpin, goby, sea robin
Primarily designed for: Redfish
Also effective on: Sea trout, flounder, bluefish
Submitted by: Greg Miheve, Master Fly Tier (Ft. Walton Beach, Florida)
Originated by: Greg Miheve
Tied by: Greg Miheve

Hook: Mustad 34007 or TMC 800S, #2/0-#4; shank bent 45-degrees toward hook point 1/4" behind eye
Thread: Fluorescent orange Flat waxed nylon
Tail: Rust Zonker strip, 2 1/2 times shank length, mottled on hide with brown marker, flanked by 5-7 strands each of gold Flashabou and copper Krystal Flash on each side
Pectoral fins: 1 russet pheasant body feather, 1 1/4 times hook gap in length, flared outward on each side of tail
Body: 3 orange grizzly hackles, thickly palmered
Shellback: Orange Mylar tubing
Eyes: Nickel-plated brass with painted black pupils

Bottom view

Comments: This fly is also effective in olive, tan, chinchilla, white, dyed brown, natural brown, and chartreuse.

Hart Grass Shrimp

Overall length: 4" on #4 hook
Pattern type: Grass shrimp
Primarily designed for: Speckled sea trout
Also effective on: Redfish, bonefish
Submitted by: Brazos Fly Fishers (Granbury, Texas)
Originated by: Richard Hart
Tied by: Richard Hart

Hook: Partridge CS54 shrimp or Mustad 34011, #4
Thread: White Danville Flat waxed nylon
Weed guard: 12-lb. Mason hard nylon
Antennae & mouthparts: Pearl Krystal Flash
Eyes: Jalapeno colored Killer Caddis beads glued to 30-lb. Mason hard nylon
Shellback: White Swiss straw
Body: Light olive dun Antron dubbing
Legs: White saddle hackle
Tail: White Swiss Straw from shellback

Hidalgo's Bride of Hardhead

Overall length: 3 1/2" on #1/0 hook
Pattern type: General attractor; baitfish imitation in appropriate colors
Primarily designed for: Redfish
Also effective on: Sea trout, snook
Submitted by: The Fly Shop (Fort Lauderdale, Florida)
Originated by: Carlos Hidalgo
Tied by: Carlos Hidalgo

Chartreuse/white version

Hook: Mustad 34007, #1/0; front 1/3 of shank bent away from hook point; rear of hook weighted with lead wire
Thread: Black size A
Tail: Red Flashabou (none on chartreuse/white version)
Body: Red Poly Flash or Diamond Braid
Wing: Black Krystal Flash over black bucktail flanked by 1 grizzly neck hackle feather per side flanked by 1 black neck hackle feather per side (for chartreuse/white version: peacock herl over chartreuse Flashabou over silver Krystal Flash over white bucktail, flanked by 1 grizzly neck hackle feather per side)
Head: Black chenille (chartreuse chenille for chartreuse/white version) cover with 2 coats of 5-minute epoxy
Eyes: Prismatic Stick-on eyes

Hidalgo's Flash Minnow

Overall length: 2" on #1/0 hook
Pattern type: Glass minnow
Primarily designed for: Snook
Also effective on: Jacks
Submitted by: The Fly Shop (Fort Lauderdale, Florida)
Originated by: Carlos Hidalgo
Tied by: Carlos Hidalgo

Blue version

Hook: Mustad 34007, #3/0-#2
Thread: Chartreuse size A (black for blue version)
Body: Pearl Krystal Flash (rainbow Krystal Flash for blue version) overwrapped with clear flexible plastic tubing or cord such as Larva Lace, Jelly Cord, Swannundaze, or nylon monofilament
Wing: Chartreuse Flashabou (blue Flashabou for blue version)
Head: Tying thread coated with 5-minute epoxy
Eyes: Painted, white with black pupils

Comments: This pattern can be tied in many color combinations, but the chartreuse version is particularly effective.

Hidalgo's Hardhead

Bicolor version

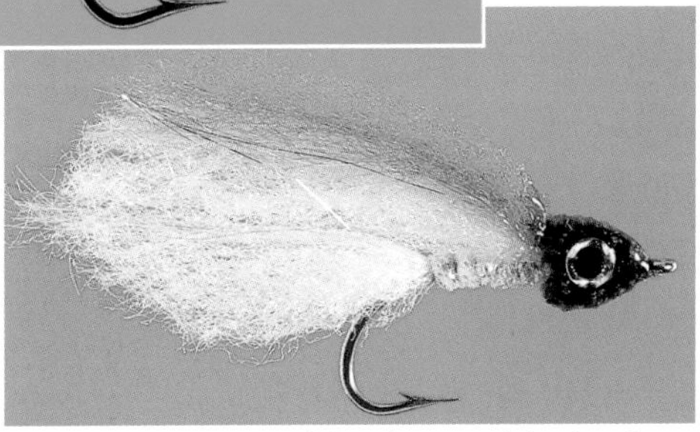

Overall length: 2 1/2" on #1/0 hook
Pattern type: General attractor; baitfish imitation in appropriate colors
Primarily designed for: Snook
Also effective on: Jacks
Submitted by: The Fly Shop (Fort Lauderdale, Florida)
Originated by: Carlos Hidalgo
Tied by: Carlos Hidalgo

Hook: Mustad 34007, #3/0-#2
Thread: Yellow size A (green for bicolor version)
Tail: Yellow "The Fuzz" topped with yellow Lite Brite (white "The Fuzz" topped with polar bear Lite Brite for bicolor version)
Wing: Yellow "The Fuzz" over yellow Lite Brite over yellow "The Fuzz" (green "The Fuzz" over silver Lite Brite over white "The Fuzz" for bicolor version)
Head: Yellow chenille (green for bicolor version) coated with 5-minute epoxy
Eyes: Prismatic Stick-on eyes

Comments: Any fine synthetic fiber can be substituted for "The Fuzz" on this pattern. When finishing the head, apply epoxy completely over the chenille and into the base of the wing fibers; this will help the wing hold its shape in the water. When the epoxy is hardened, apply a second coat over the chenille to make it smooth.

Hidalgo's Mara-Ducer

Orange version

Overall length: 3 1/2" on #1 hook
Pattern type: General attractor
Primarily designed for: Redfish
Also effective on: Sea trout, jacks, snook
Submitted by: The Fly Shop (Fort Lauderdale, Florida)
Originated by: Carlos Hidalgo
Tied by: Carlos Hidalgo

Hook: Mustad 34007, #1
Thread: Black size A (orange for orange version)
Tail: Brown marabou with gold Flashabou on each side (peach marabou with pearl Flashabou for orange version)
Body: Brown neck hackle palmered over length of shank followed by grizzly hackle at front of body (orange hackle along entire shank for orange version)

Comments: This variation of a Sea-Ducer uses a marabou tail for better action in the water. It is a good shallow-water fly that can be fished right along the surface or allowed to sink a bit. It can be tied in various color combinations.

Hidalgo's Polar Aire Streamer

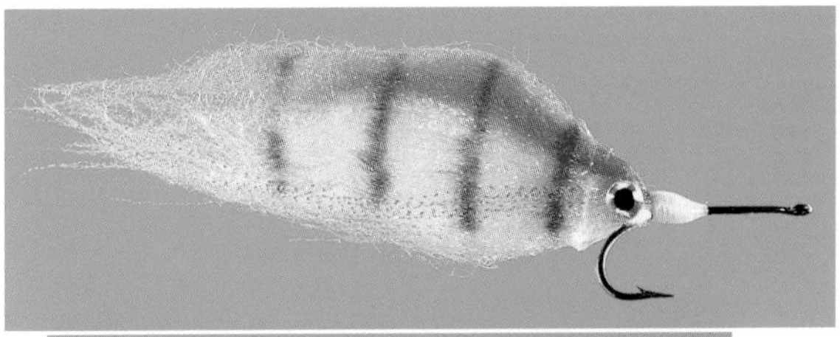

Tri-color version

Overall length: 6" on #3/0
Pattern type: General attractor; baitfish imitation in appropriate colors
Primarily designed for: Snook
Also effective on: Jacks
Submitted by: The Fly Shop (Fort Lauderdale, Florida)
Originated by: Carlos Hidalgo
Tied by: Carlos Hidalgo

Hook: Mustad 34007, #3/0-#2
Thread: Yellow size A (green for tricolor version)
Wing: Fluorescent orange Polar Aire over yellow Polar Aire; vertical markings added with orange water proof marker (tricolor version: oliver Polar Aire over gray Polar Aire over white Polar Aire)
Lateral line: Yellow Krystal Flash (pearl Krystal Flash on tricolor version)
Eyes: Prismatic Stick-on eyes
Head: 5-minute epoxy

Comments: This fly can be tied in a variety of color combinations. Carlos Hidalgo notes that the way epoxy is applied to the head of this fly is crucial. Spread the wing fibers with thumb and forefinger, and apply epoxy to the thread head, eyes, and the front portion of the wing, extending back behind the eye. Applying the epoxy in this way keeps the wing fibers spread out for a better action in the water.

Hidalgo's Son of Hardhead

Overall length: 3 1/4" on #1 hook
Pattern type: General attractor; baitfish imitation in appropriate colors
Primarily designed for: Snook
Also effective on: Jacks
Submitted by: The Fly Shop (Fort Lauderdale, Florida)
Originated by: Carlos Hidalgo
Tied by: Carlos Hidalgo

Hook: Mustad 34011, #2/0-#4; lead-wire weight optional
Thread: Red size A (yellow for yellow version)
Body: Pearl Poly Flash or Diamond Braid (yellow for yellow version)
Wing: Red bucktail over red Krystal Flash over white bucktail, flanked by 1 grizzly neck hackle per side (yellow version: green bucktail over yellow Krystal Flash over yellow bucktail, flanked by 1 yellow grizzly neck hackle per side)
Head: Red chenille (yellow chenille colored on top with green marker for yellow version), covered with 2 coats of 5-minute epoxy
Eyes: Prismatic Stick-on eyes

Yellow version

Hidalgo's Trout Teaser

Overall length: 3" on #1/0 hook
Pattern type: General attractor
Primarily designed for: Sea trout
Also effective on: Jacks, snook, redfish
Submitted by: The Fly Shop (Fort Lauderdale, Florida)
Originated by: Carlos Hidalgo
Tied by: Carlos Hidalgo

Hook: Mustad 34007, #1/0; bent back 1/3 shank length behind eye; weight optional
Thread: Red size A (cerise for cerise version; chartreuse for chartreuse version)
Body: Red chenille (cerise for cerise version; chartreuse for chartreuse version)
Wing: Red Krystal Flash over gold Krystal Flash over red bucktail (cerise version: cerise Krystal Flash over rainbow Krystal Flash over cerise bucktail; chartreuse version: chartreuse Krystal Flash over silver Krystal Flash over chartreuse bucktail)
Head: Tying thread coated with 5-minute epoxy
Eyes: Painted, white with black pupils

Cerise version

Chartreuse version

Comments: This is a very simple fly to tie. The red version was designed for Florida Bay (out of Flamingo); the cerise for Biscayne Bay, and the chartreuse for the Indian River.

Hidalgo's Vampire

Overall length: 3 1/4" on #2 hook
Pattern type: Glass minnow
Primarily designed for: Snook
Also effective on: Baby tarpon, sea trout
Submitted by: The Fly Shop (Fort Lauderdale, Florida)
Originated by: Carlos Hidalgo
Tied by: Carlos Hidalgo

Hook: Mustad 34011, #1/0-#4
Thread: White size A
Body: Pearl Poly Flash or Diamond Braid
Wing: Polar bear Lite Brite over white bucktail
Head: White thread coated with 5-minute epoxy
Eyes: Painted, yellow with black pupils

Comments: This fly, says originator Carlos Hidalgo, was designed for fishing snook at night around lighted docks, but is useful wherever glass minnows are found.

Key Lime Fly

Overall length: 3" on 2/0 hook
Pattern type: Shrimp
Primarily designed for: Tarpon, bonefish
Also effective on: Snook, permit
Submitted by: Key West Angler (Key West, Florida)
Originated by: John O'Hearn and Bryan Yates
Tied by: John O'Hearn

Hook: Gamakatsu SC15, #2/0-#2
Thread: Chartreuse Gudebrod size G
Tail spreader: Chartreuse calf tail topped with 6-8 long badger guard hairs and 2-3 strands of pearl Krystal Flash
Tail: One wide chartreuse neck hackle flanked by 2 wide grizzly neck hackles on each side, tied splayed
Collar: Natural badger body fur followed by grizzly hackle
Head: Tying thread coated with epoxy

Top view

Comments: John O'Hearn notes that this fly is most effective when tied small (2 1/2" to 3") and fished over hard green bottoms to laid-up tarpon.

Lawler Crawler

Overall length: 4" on #2 hook
Pattern type: Shrimp
Primarily designed for: Redfish, speckled sea trout
Also effective on: Striped bass
Submitted by: Shrevetown Trading Company Fly Shop (Shreveport, Louisiana)
Originated by: Paul Lawler
Tied by: Carol Bernstein

Top view

Hook: Mustad 34007, #2-#6
Thread: Danville Fine Monofilament
Legs: White schlappen or bass/saltwater hackle, palmered; clipped on top and sides
Shellback: Pink Flashabou Accent or Krystal Flash, coated with epoxy and drawn to shape, epoxied to top of shank
Eyes: Bug Eyes
Antennae: Moose mane fibers

Lord Pinky

Overall length: 1 1/2" on #6 hook
Pattern type: General attractor
Primarily designed for: Redfish
Also effective on: Sea trout, bonefish
Submitted by: Padre Outfitters (South Padre Island, Texas)
Originated by: Bill Hagen
Tied by: Bill Hagen

Top view

Hook: Mustad 34007, #4-#6
Thread: Pink Flymaster Plus
Weed guard: 15-lb. hard Mason monofilament
Tail: Pink calf tail flanked by one pink neck hackle on each side, tied splayed
Body: Pink Orvis Dragon Fur
Eyes: Non-toxic barbell eyes, small

Comments: Tyer Bill Hagen explains, "Tied in size 6, this is an excellent fly for shallow waters, less than a foot deep. Deeper waters require heavier barbell eyes. Pink is an excellent color for redfish, while tan and lighter colors (depending on bottom color) work well for bonefish. This patterns was designed for situations when redfish are extremely shallow and presentation must be soft. It matches the size of young shrimp and baitfish which inhabit the skinny water of secondary bays in Laguna Madre. It's very reliable."

Matt's 40

Overall length: 4 1/2" on #1 hook
Pattern type: Baitfish
Primarily designed for: Snook, redfish, tarpon
Also effective on: Jacks, mackerel
Submitted by: Everglades Angler (Naples, Florida)
Originated by: Matt Hoover
Tied by: Matt Hoover

Hook: Mustad 34007, #3/0-#1
Thread: Black Danville Flat waxed nylon
Wing: Peacock herl over one clump olive or green marabou over one clump white marabou on each side of shank, flanked by 2 white neck hackles on each side
Head: Tying thread
Eyes: White Prism Eyes
Weed guard: Wire, tied Mullendore style

Comments: In this pattern, the feathers in the wing should be tied with concave sides together so that the feathers curve toward one another and downward. They should be 1/2" to 3/4" longer than the marabou to allow them to "swim." Epoxy around the head and eyes, but not over the eyes themselves, as the epoxy will cloud them.

M.C.B.E.S.L.T

Overall length: 2 1/2" on #2/0 hook
Pattern type: General attractor
Effective on: Snook, redfish, speckled sea trout
Submitted by: Swann's Fly Shop (Dade City, Florida)
Originated by: Jim Swann
Tied by: Jim Swann

Hook: VMC Gold, #2/0
Thread: White
Weed guard: Double strand of monofilament
Mouthparts: Tan marabou over black bucktail
Claws: 2 badger saddle hackles
Eyes: Black plastic bead chain
Legs: Badger saddle hackle, wrapped
Underbody: Closed-cell foam
Overbody: Pearlescent Mylar tubing sleeved over underbody

Bottom view

Comments: The name of this pattern, pronounced "McBeslt", stands for "minnow, crayfish, bug-eyed-shrimp, looking thing."

The Menhaden

Overall length: 4" on #2/0 hook
Pattern type: Atlantic menhaden
Primarily designed for: Snook, tarpon, striped bass
Also effective on: Sea trout, barracuda, permit, redfish, and other species
Submitted by: The Back Country, Inc. (Vero Beach, Florida)
Originated by: Captain Eric T. Davis version of Polafibre Minnow
Tied by: Captain Eric T. Davis

Hook: Gamakatsu SC15, #2/0-#2
Thread: Clear Mono Thread
Tail: White Polafibre
Gills: Red Polafibre
Wing: Olive Polafibre over chartreuse Polafibre over white Polafibre; strands of pearl Flashabou and chartreuse Fluorofibre enclosed in white Polafibre; markings added with permanent marker
Lateral accents: Root beer Comes Alive on top; pearl Flashabou on sides
Eyes: 3-D Molded eyes, large

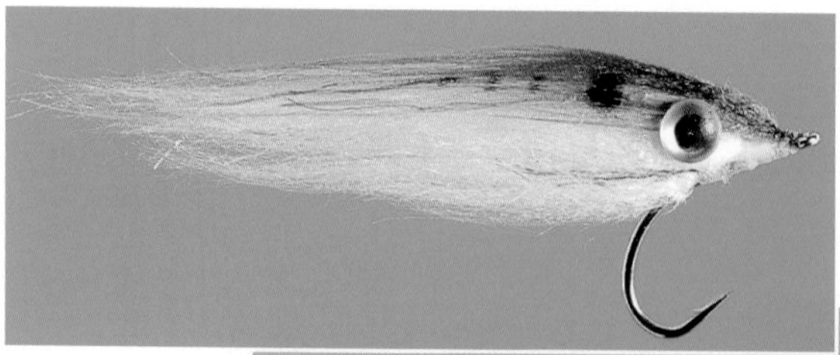

Top view

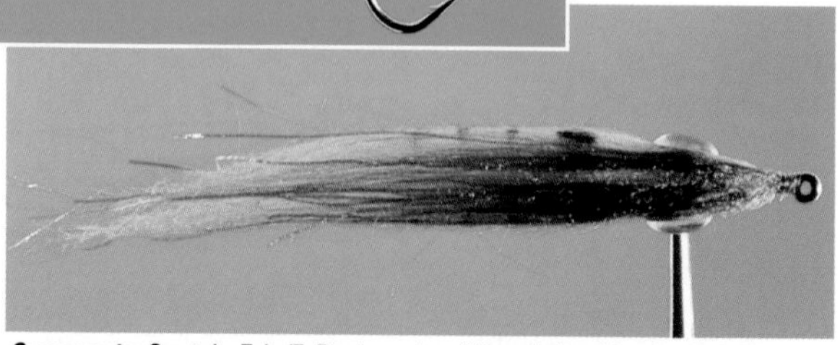

Comments: Captain Eric T. Davis notes, "Popularized by the Polafibre Minnow style, this fly is a great baitfish representation. The addition of Fluorofibre and Flashabou inside the Polafibre wing makes the fly very translucent, giving it almost an internal flash. The red gills makes the fly appear hurt or wounded—easy prey for the predator. The hook rides in a deadly position, and this fly has an excellent hook-up ratio on tarpon. Tied in other color combinations, the fly can imitate other baitfish—mullet, sardine, anchovy, butterfish, herring, or just about anything."

Mess of a Crab

Top view

Overall length: 2 3/4" on #4 hook
Pattern type: Crab, shrimp
Primarily designed for: Bonefish, permit
Also effective on: Snapper, sea trout, snook, sheepshead, flounder, redfish
Submitted by: The Back Country, Inc. (Vero Beach, Florida)
Originated by: Paul Ringold
Tied by: Paul Ringold

Hook: Mustad 34007, #4-#6
Thread: 2-lb. Ande clear monofilament
Antennae: 2 strands black Ultra Hair
Mouthparts: Tan/brown bucktail
Claws: 2 ginger variant hackle tips, tied splayed
Body: Tan leech yarn
Legs: Tan Life Flex rubber legs, marked with brown permanent marker
Eyes: Black extra-large bead chain
Weed guard: Clear monofilament

Comments: This pattern is also effective tied in olive, brown, sand, and black.

Mr. Pinky

Overall length: 2" on #4 hook
Pattern type: General attractor
Primarily designed for: Redfish
Also effective on: Sea trout, bonefish
Submitted by: Padre Outfitters (South Padre Island, Texas)
Originated by: Captain Eric Glass
Tied by: Captain Eric Glass version of Chico Fernandez Bendback

Hook: TMC 811S, #4-#6
Thread: Black Danville Plus
Body: Fluorescent pink chenille, medium
Wing: Dark hair from center of red-dyed bucktail, flanked by 4 strands red Flashabou on each side

Comments: Captain Glass notes, "This is an excellent fly on bright days for tailing redfish. It works best when placed very close to a tailing fish and stripped fairly briskly away; use about 20" strips. It's simple to tie, and I get ribbed a lot by my friends because it's gaudy, and doesn't have eyes, legs, antennae, etc. But the local redfish love it, and I've watched several hundred different clients catch fish with it. So it's a wheel I'm reluctant to re-invent."

Mullet Diver

Top view

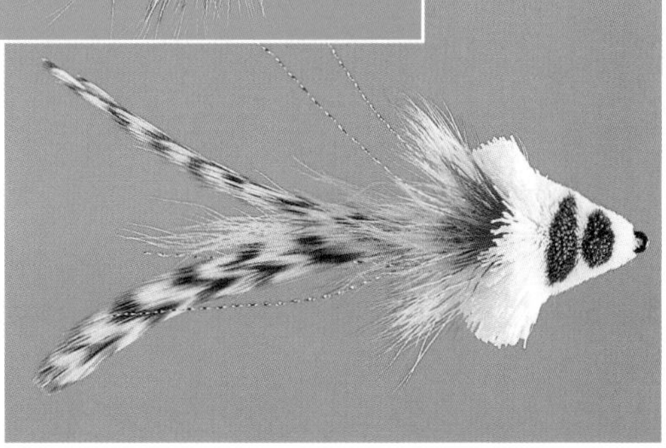

Overall length: 3 1/4" on #2 hook
Pattern type: Injured mullet
Primarily designed for: Snook, sea trout
Also effective on: All shallow-water species
Submitted by: The Back Country, Inc. (Vero Beach, Florida)
Originated by: Version of Larry Dahlberg's Diver
Tied by: John Fuchs

Hook: Mustad 3366, #2
Thread: Mono for tail; single-strand floss for stacking deer hair
Tail: White bucktail
Wing: Tuft of gray marabou over 2 grizzly hackles on each side of tail, flanked by 2 strands silver Krystal Flash on each side
Collar: Grizzly neck hackle, palmered
Head: White, pink, and blue deer hair, stacked and clipped

Needlefish

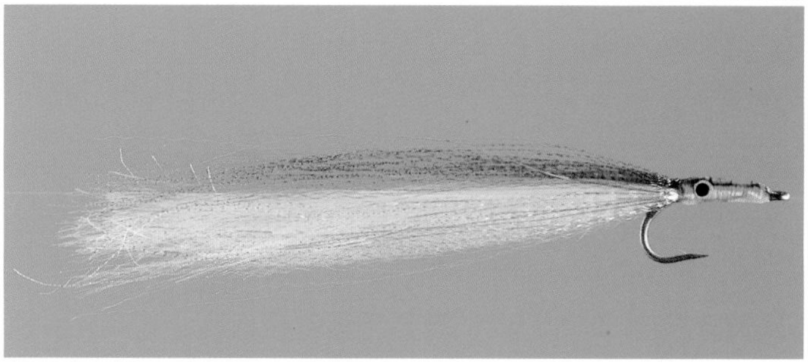

Overall length: 5 3/4" on #1/0 hook
Pattern type: Needlefish, balao
Primarily designed for: Barracuda
Also effective on: Jacks, bluefish, mackerel
Submitted by: Greg Miheve, Master Fly Tier (Ft. Walton Beach, Florida)
Originated by: Greg Miheve adaptation of standard needlefish patterns
Tied by: Greg Miheve

Hook: Standard saltwater, #3/0-#2
Thread: White Flat waxed nylon
Tail: Green Krystal Flash over green Ultra Hair over chartreuse Flashabou over chartreuse Ultra Hair over pearl Flashabou over white Ultra Hair
Body: Tying thread wrapped over butts of tail material, colored on top with green permanent marker and on sides with chartreuse marker; coated with epoxy
Gills: Red thread wrapped 1/3 way around hook bend, lacquered

Comments: Greg Miheve notes, "Many of my clients purchase this pattern with 5" of #3 wire attached to the hook with a Haywire Twist and a loop at the other end for a 'pocket 'cuda kit' to carry when wading for bonefish—they just cut off the bone fly, tie on this one, and hold on. Alternate colors are: dark blue/light blue/white, all chartreuse, orange, black, white."

One Shot Crab

Top view

Overall length: 2" on #4 hook
Pattern type: Crab
Primarily designed for: Bonefish, permit
Also effective on: Mutton snapper, sea trout, sheepshead, snook, redfish
Submitted by: The Back Country, Inc. (Vero Beach, Florida)
Originated by: Paul Ringold
Tied by: Paul Ringold

Hook: Mustad 34007, #4; Mustad 7766, #1/0; weighted with black plastic barbell eyes behind hook eye
Thread: 2-lb. Ande clear monofilament
Mouthparts: Brown bucktail mixed with pearl Krystal Flash
Claws: 2 tan grizzly hackle tips, tied splayed
Hackle: Grizzly
Eyes: Permit 1/0 monofilament, melted and flattened at ends; red prismatic eyes glued to flattened mono, then dipped in clear epoxy
Body: Tan sculpin wool, stacked and clipped

Comments: This pattern is also good tied in olive, dark brown, and black. When tying the body, put pencil-sized pieces of wool on either side of the hook, as if stacking deer hair. Bind both pieces down simultaneously. Apply head cement to wrappings. On larger hooks, additional pieces of wool may be necessary.

Polafibre Whistler

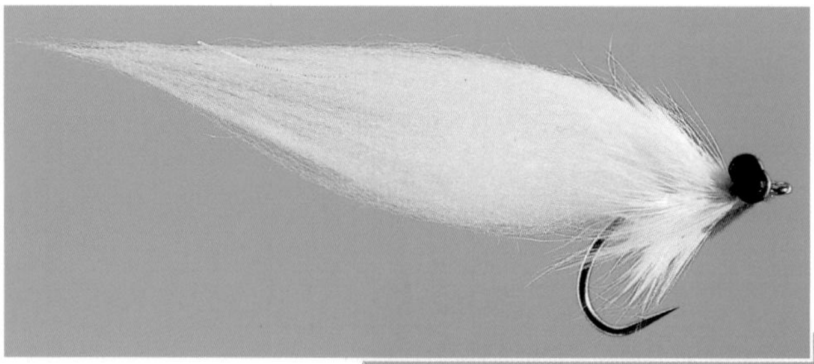

Olive/white version

Overall length: 3 3/4" on #2/0 hook
Pattern type: General attractor, shrimp, minnow
Primarily designed for: Tarpon, snook
Also effective on: Trout, snapper, jacks, dolphin, kingfish, mackerel, and most predatory species
Submitted by: The Back Country, Inc. (Vero Beach, Florida)
Originated by: Version of Dan Blanton's Whistler
Tied by: Paul Ringold

Hook: Mustad 34007 or Gamakatsu SC-15, #2/0-#1/0
Thread: 2-lb. Ande clear monofilament
Wing: White Polafibre mixed with a few strands pearl Fire Fly (olive Polafibre over red Fire Fly over white Polafibre for olive/white version)
Collar: White hackle (olive hackle for olive/white version)
Gills: Orange Fluorofibre
Eyes: Black extra-large bead chain

Comments: To prevent fouling, pull the wing fibers slightly upward and dab Softex at the base to stiffen. This fly fishes well without eyes, as a Sea-Ducer pattern.

Rabbit Bend Back

Overall length: 2 1/4" on #1 hook
Pattern type: Snapping shrimp
Primarily designed for: Redfish
Also effective on: Sea trout
Submitted by: The Back Country, Inc. (Vero Beach, Florida)
Originated by: Adaptation of Chico's Bendback
Tied by: Captain Eric T. Davis

Hook: Mustad 34007, #2/0-#2
Thread: Black 3/0 Monocord
Body: Orange chenille
Wing: 2 cree or variegated hackles over gold Flashabou over brown bucktail
Collar: Brown rabbit fur, one wrap

Comments: Captain Davis notes that this is an excellent searching pattern for blind casting into the mangroves. The wing materials make the fly weedless, and it has a very quiet entry into the water. The pattern can also be weighted with lead wire to run deeper into the weeds.

Rattle Belly Hot Lips

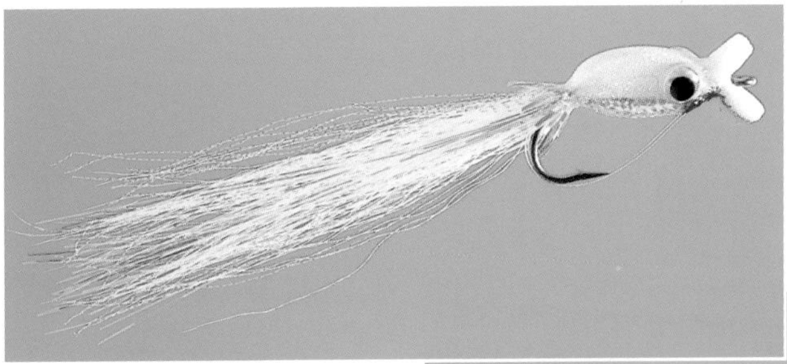

Bottom view

Overall length: 5" on #2/0 hook
Pattern type: Floating wounded baitfish
Primarily designed for: Snook
Also effective on: Speckled sea trout, bluefish, striped bass
Submitted by: Greg Miheve, Master Fly Tier (Ft. Walton Beach, Florida)
Originated by: Greg Miheve adaptation of Steve Huff design
Tied by: Greg Miheve

Hook: TMC 811S or VMC9255PS or Mustad 34007 or 3407, #2/0
Thread: White Flat waxed nylon
Weed guard: 20-lb. Mason hard mono
Tail: Pearl Krystal Flash over white bucktail flanked by pearl Flashabou
Underbody: Rattle sleeved in pearl Mylar tubing and tied to underside of shank
Overbody: Strip of white closed-cell foam tied in middle atop shank at tailing point, then folded forward and tied off at hook eye to form top and bottom lips. Glue foam with thinned Goop between layers and to top of underbody. Trim lips to shape. Underside of lower lip colored red with permanent marker.
Eyes: 7mm white doll eyes with black pupil, glued with thinned Goop

Comments: Greg Miheve notes that a long-shank hook can be used to provide a sleeker profile and more flotation, since more foam is used in the body. The doll eyes add a little more floatation and rattle. He continues, "Substituting silver for pearl in the all-white version produces a very different fly; adding a natural, green, or blue grizzly hackle changes it as well. An all-chartreuse version is always good, as are green over white, blue over white, and black over white. All black is good at night. After that, imagination is the only limit. Ted Juracsik really likes these on his snook trips into the Everglades."

Rattle Crab

Bottom view

Overall length: 1 3/4" on #2 hook
Pattern type: Crab
Primarily designed for: Redfish, permit
Submitted by: Brazos Fly Fishers (Granbury, Texas)
Originated by: Richard Hart
Tied by: Richard Hart

Hook: Mustad 34007, #2
Thread: Olive Danville Flat waxed nylon
Weed guard: 12-lb. Mason hard nylon
Body: 1/8" Flexo Tubing colored with Pantone marker, with 5mm Pyrex rattle glued to side of shank
Legs: Black Living Rubber, inserted into body tubing and glued
Claws: Golden pheasant shoulder coated with Softex, inserted into body tubing and glued
Eyes: Jalapeno colored Killer Caddis beads glued to 30-lb. Mason hard nylon

Rattle Mullet

Bottom view

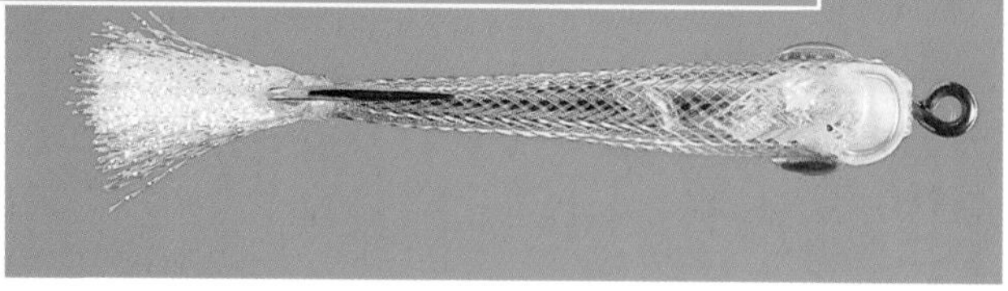

Overall length: 3 1/4" on #2/0 hook
Pattern type: Mullet
Primarily designed for: Tarpon, snook
Submitted by: Brazos Fly Fishers (Granbury, Texas)
Originated by: Richard Hart
Tied by: Richard Hart

Hook: Mustad 90233S, #2/0
Thread: White Danville Flat waxed nylon
Tail: Pearl Krystal Flash
Body: Clear 1/4" Flexo Tubing colored with Pantone markers, with 5mm Pyrex rattle glued on the underside of the front of the shank to act as keel weight
Lip: Loop of 30-lb. Mason hard nylon glued to body then dipped in Softex to form a film inside loop
Eyes: 3D Molded eyes

Red-Eye Bone

Bottom view

Overall length: 2 3/4" on #4 hook
Pattern type: Grass shrimp
Primarily designed for: Bonefish
Also effective on: Redfish, permit, small tarpon
Submitted by: Capt. Harry's Fishing Supply (Miami, Florida)
Originated by: Jesus Quintino
Tied by: Jesus Quintino

Hook: TMC 800S, #4
Thread: Tan 3/0 Monocord
Tail: 4 strands pearl Flash Accent over rust Fly Fur
Hackle: Brown saddle hackle, long
Body: Large gold tinsel coated with 5-minute epoxy
Eyes: 6mm orange plastic eyes
Weed guard: Mason 20-lb. nylon

Slam-A-Roo

Top view

Overall length: 1 1/2" on #2 hook
Pattern type: Swimming crab
Primarily designed for: Permit
Also effective on: Bonefish, redfish, and crab-eating species
Submitted by: Sea Boots Outfitters (Big Pine Key, Florida)
Originated by: Captain Lenny Moffo
Tied by: Captain Lenny Moffo

Hook: Mustad 34007, #1/0-#4
Thread: Brown 3/0 Monocord
Butt: Peacock herl or chenille
Eyes: Wapsi lead barbell eyes, size according to desired sink rate
Legs: Light tan rubber striped with brown permanent marker
Body: Alternating bands of gray, brown, and tan deer hair, spun and clipped
Weed guard (optional): 10-lb. Maxima Chameleon, striped with permanent marker

Comments: "This pattern," says Lenny Moffo, "was devised for fishing in the Lower Keys, where permit and bonefish frequent the same flats. Keys bonefish are big and eat surprisingly large flies compared to bonefish at other destinations."

Tarpon Crab
(Black and Purple)

Top view

Overall length: 3″ on #4/0 hook
Pattern type: Crab
Primarily designed for: Tarpon
Submitted by: Boca Grande Outfitters (Boca Grande, Florida)
Originated by: Unknown
Tied by: Zeke Sieglaff

Hook: Owner AKI, #5/0-#1/0
Thread: Black Flat waxed nylon
Tail: Wine marabou, flanked by 3 strands purple Flashabou per side, flanked by 3 black rooster hackles per side
Eyes: Gold glass bead with black pupils epoxied to 60-lb. mono
Body: 2 purple grizzly hackles wrapped in front of tail; purple and black deer hair, spun and clipped flat top and bottom

Ted Haas's Greenie

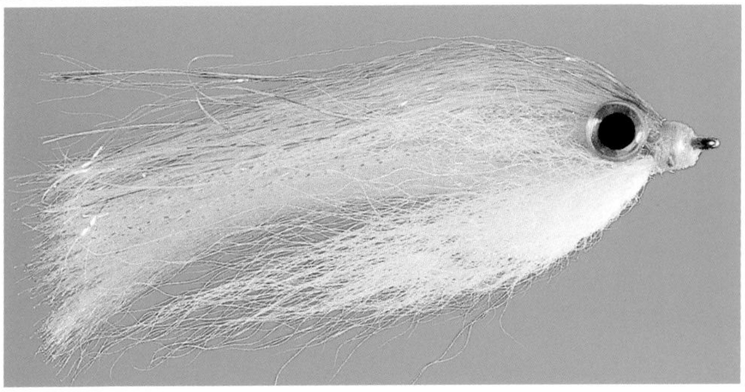

Overall length: 3″ on #1/0 hook
Pattern type: Greenback, sardine, pilchard
Primarily designed for: Snook
Also effective on: Sea trout, redfish, ladyfish, small tarpon
Submitted by: Swann's Fly Shop (Dade City, Florida)
Originated by: Ted Haas
Tied by: Ted Haas

Hook: Mustad stainless steel, #1/0
Thread: White Flat waxed nylon
Body: White Flat waxed nylon
Wing: Light green Flashabou over pearl Krystal Flash over white Supreme Hair
Belly: White arctic fox fur
Eyes: Stick-on eyes, holographic chartreuse

Ted Haas's Tan 'N' White

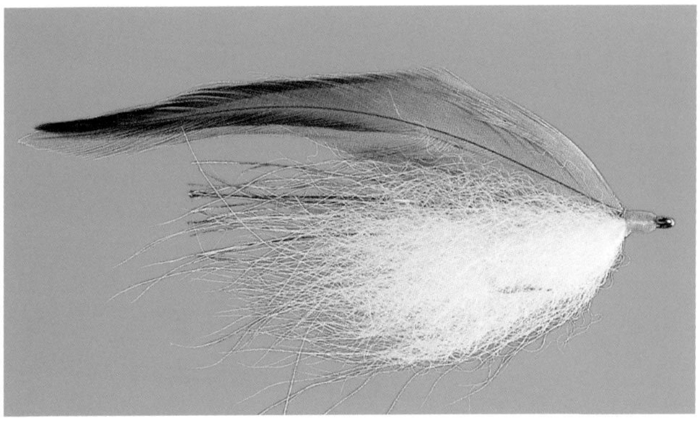

Overall length: 3 1/4″ on #4 hook
Pattern type: Anchovy, baitfish
Primarily designed for: Snook, redfish
Also effective on: Sea trout, ladyfish
Submitted by: Swann's Fly Shop (Dade City, Florida)
Originated by: Ted Haas
Tied by: Ted Haas

Hook: Mustad stainless steel, #4
Thread: White Danville Flat waxed nylon
Tail: Gold Flashabou
Body: Gold Flashabou, wrapped
Wing: 2 tan saddle hackles
Belly: White arctic fox fur

3-D Stand-Up Clouser

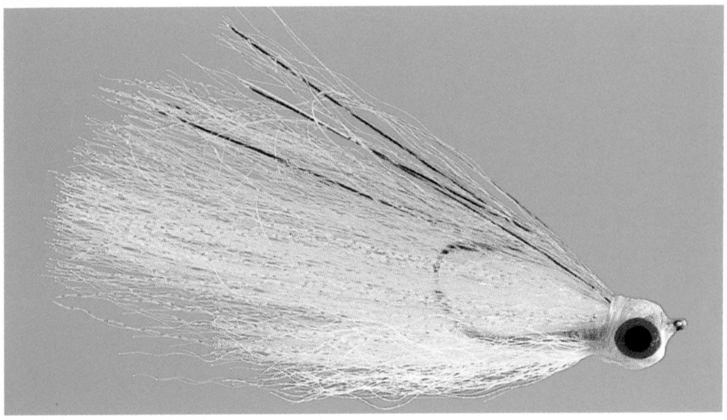

Overall length: 2 3/4″ on #2 hook
Pattern type: Minnow, greenback, pinfish
Primarily designed for: Redfish, snook, tarpon
Also effective on: Ladyfish, jacks
Submitted by: Swann's Fly Shop (Dade City, Florida)
Originated by: Adaptation of Bob Clouser design
Tied by: Ted Haas

Hook: Mustad stainless steel, #2
Thread: White Danville Flat Waxed 3/0
Wing: Green Flashabou over chartreuse Supreme Hair over white Supreme Hair; flanked with pearl Krystal Flash
Belly: White bucktail over white Supreme Hair
Eyes: Lead barbell painted red with black pupils

Up/Down Pin Fish

Top view

Overall length: 4" on #3/0 hook
Pattern type: Pin fish
Primarily designed for: All saltwater species
Submitted by: The Back Country, Inc. (Vero Beach, Florida)
Originated by: John Fuchs
Tied by: John Fuchs

Hook: Mustad 34007, #3/0
Thread: Mono
Tail: White bucktail
Belly: White bucktail, staggered on underside of shank
Wing: Peacock herl over tan bucktail over yellow Krystal Flash over tan bucktail over pink bucktail over gold Comes Alive over yellow bucktail over white bucktail, flanked with gold Lite Brite; vertical bars added with permanent black marker
Gills: Red calf tail
Eyes: 7mm holographic eyes, gold with black pupils
Head: 30-minute epoxy

Utility Minnow

Comments: This fly is easy to tie and Captain Lenny Moffo says he carries it in an assortment of sizes; it works on anything eats baitfish.

Overall length: 3" on #2/0 hook
Pattern type: Baitfish
Primarily designed for: Small tarpon
Also effective on: Snook, spotted sea trout, sharks, barracuda
Submitted by: Sea Boots Outfitters (Big Pine Key, Florida)
Originated by: Captain Lenny Moffo
Tied by: Captain Lenny Moffo

Hook: Gamakatsu SC-15, #3/0-#2; weight with lead wire optional
Thread: Chartreuse 3/0 Monocord
Tail: Chartreuse bucktail over gold Flashabou over white bucktail
Lateral line: Brown grizzly neck hackle
Wing: 4 strands peacock herl over chartreuse bucktail over white bucktail
Belly: White bucktail
Head: Orange 3/0 Flat-waxed thread
Eyes: Witchcraft tape eyes; coat head and eyes with 5-minute epoxy

Weighted Bend Back

Bottom view

Overall length: 1 3/4" on #4 hook
Pattern type: General attractor
Primarily designed for: Bonefish
Also effective on: Snook, redfish, speckled sea trout
Submitted by: Swann's Fly Shop (Dade City, Florida)
Originated by: Unknown
Tied by: Jim Swann

Hook: Mustad 34007, #2-#8; bent 30 degrees away from hook point behind hook eye, bend back style
Thread: Chartreuse
Eyes: Lead barbell, painted white with black pupils, coated with epoxy
Wing: Pearl Flashabou over chartreuse FisHair over white FisHair
Body: Chartreuse glitter epoxy

Contributor Information

• CONNECTICUT •

Housatonic River Outfitters, Inc.
Rt. 128
P.O. Box 228
West Cornwall, CT 06786
Mail order: Flies, materials, tackle; catalog (free)
Information and orders: (860) 672-1010 (phone and fax)
Online information/catalog: www.dryflies.com
E-mail: hflyshop@aol.com
Patterns: Rube's Anchovy, p. 77
Rube's Blushing Wide Fly, p. 46
Rube's Wounded Baby Bunker, p. 46

Northrop's Landing
520 Riverside Ave.
Westport, CT 06880
Mail order: Flies, materials, tackle
Information and orders: (203) 226-1915; fax (203) 454-0857
Online information/catalog: www.saltwater-flyfishing.com
E-mail: godzilla41@aol.com
Patterns: Bozo Hair Bunker, p. 29
Green Molly, p. 41

• FLORIDA •

The Back Country, Inc.
2046 Treasure Coast Plaza, Unit C
Vero Beach, FL 32960
Mail order: Flies, materials, tackle; catalog (free)
Information and orders: (561) 567-6665; fax (561) 567-6744
Online information/catalog: www.verobackcountry.com
E-mail: tbackcoun@aol.com
Patterns: B.C. Crustacean, p. 52
B.C. Shrimp, p. 52
Big Eyed Chovy, p. 53
Blue Crab, p. 54
FuzBone, p. 61
Giant Dahlberg, p. 61
Glass Minnow—Bullethead, p. 62
Mess of a Crab, p. 71
Mullet Diver, p. 71
One Shot Crab, p. 72
Polafibre Whistler, p. 72
Rabbit Bend Back, p. 73
The Menhaden, p. 70
Up/Down Pinfish, p. 76

Boca Grande Outfitters, Inc.
P.O. Box 1799
Boca Grande, FL 33921
Mail order: Flies, materials, tackle
Information and orders: (941) 964-2445; fax (941) 964-2447
E-mail: tarpon@flyfishing-florida.com
Patterns: Cole's Peel & Eat Shrimp, p. 55
Tarpon Crab (Black and Purple), p. 75

Capt. Harry's Fishing Supply
100 NE 11th St.
Miami, FL 33132
Mail order: Flies, materials, tackle; catalog (free)
Information and orders: (800) 327-4088, (305) 374-4661; fax (305) 374-3713
E-mail: www.captharry.com
Patterns: Big Boy Tarpon Shrimp, p. 53
Red-Eye Bone, p. 74

Everglades Angler
810 12th Ave. So.
Naples, FL 34102
Mail order: Flies, materials, tackle; catalog (free)
Information: (941) 262-8228; fax (941) 262-0572
Orders: (800) 573-4749
Online information/catalog: evergladesangler.com
E-mail: mail@evergladesangler.com
Patterns: Black Dog, p. 53
DT, p. 59
Matt's 40, p. 70

The Fly Shop
5130 N. Federal Hwy.
Ft. Lauderdale, FL 33319
Mail order: Materials, tackle
Information and orders: (954) 772-5822; fax, same
Online information/catalog: flyshopfl@aol.com
E-mail: flyshopfl@aol.com
Patterns: Epoxy Minnow, p. 60
Epoxy Slider, p. 60
Hidalgo's Bride of Hardhead, p. 66
Hidalgo's Flash Minnow, p. 66
Hidalgo's Hardhead, p. 67
Hidalgo's Mara-Ducer, p. 67
Hidalgo's Polar Aire Streamer, p. 67
Hidalgo's Son of Hardhead, p. 68
Hidalgo's Trout Teaser, p. 68
Hidalgo's Vampire, p. 68

Greg Miheve, Master Fly Tier
507 Dory Ave.
Ft. Walton Beach, FL 32548
Mail order: Flies; price list available (free)
Information and orders: (805) 244-1602; fax (850) 243-8659 (call before faxing)
E-mail: gmiheve@gnt.net
Patterns: Greg's Blonde, p. 64
Greg's Bottom Feeder, p. 64
Greg's Cobia Pulsar, p. 64
Greg's Flats Fly, p. 65
Greg's Redfish Furtail, p. 65
Needlefish, p. 72
Rattle Belly Hot Lips, p. 73

Key West Angler
Hilton Resort & Marina
243 Front St.
Key West, FL 33040
Mail order: Materials, tackle; catalog (free)
Information and orders: (305) 296-0700; fax (305) 296-7076
Online information/catalog: keywestangler.com
E-mail: kwstangler@aol.com
Patterns: Algal Bloom, p. 51
Key Lime Fly, p. 69

Sea Boots Outfitters
9975 OVS. Hwy. MM30 Gulfside
Big Pine Key, FL 33043
Mail order: Materials, tackle
Information and orders: (800) 238-1746; fax (305) 872-0780
Online information/catalog: www.seaboots.com
E-mail: seaboots5@aol.com
Patterns: Bone Bug, p. 54
Fleeing Crab, p. 61
Slam-A-Roo, p. 74
Utility Minnow, p. 76

Swann's Fly Shop
13650 U.S. 98 Bypass
Dade City, FL 33525
Mail order: Flies, materials, tackle
Information and orders: (352) 567-6029
Patterns: Arctic Fox Fly, p. 51
Arctic Shrimp, p. 52
Crab, p. 57
Deer Hair Saltwater Diver, p. 58
Epoxy Charlie, p. 59
Epoxy Minnow, p. 59
Glass Spoon Fly, p. 62
Gold Spoon, p. 63
Graham's Deceiver (Tan/White/Grizzly), p. 63
Graham's Finger Mullet Magnum, p. 63
Graham's Mullet (Brown Phase), p. 63
M.C.B.E.S.L.T., p. 70
Ted Haas's Greenie, p. 75
Ted Haas's Tan 'N' White, p. 75
3-D Stand-Up Clouser, p. 75
Weighted Bend Back, p. 76

• GEORGIA •

The Fish Hawk
279 Buckhead Ave.
Atlanta, GA 30305
Mail order: Flies, materials, tackle
Information and orders: (404) 237-3473; fax (404) 233-5065
Online: thefishawk.com
Patterns: Cowen's Coyote, p. 55
Cowen's E-Z Body Baitfish, p. 56
Cowen's Magnum Bunker, p. 56
Cowen's Magnum Herring, p. 56
Cowen's Swimming Mini-Menhadden, p. 57

• LOUISIANA •

Shrevetown Trading Company Fly Shop
6505 Line Ave., #8
Shreveport, LA 71106
Mail order: Flies, materials, tackle
Information and orders: (318) 868-8651
Patterns: Don's Popping Shrimp, p. 59
Lawler Crawler, p. 69

• MAINE •

The Fly Fisherman's Place
57 Beechwood St.
Thomaston, ME 04861
Mail order: Flies, materials, tackle
Information and orders: (207) 354-8148; fax, same
E-mail: dartnall@midcoast.com
Patterns: Walsh Schoolie, p. 21

Eldredge Bros. Fly Shop
P.O. Box 69, Rt. 1
Cape Neddick, ME 03902
Mail order: Flies, materials, tackle; catalog (free)
Information and orders: (207) 363-9269; fax (207) 363-9287
Online information/catalog: eldredgeflyshop.com
E-mail: ebflyshop@cybertours.com
Patterns: Benoit's Patriot Popper, p. 9
Benoit's Virtual Baitfish, p. 10
Emmons Bozo Herring, p. 12
Emmons Bozo Mackerel, p. 12
Emmons Sandy Eel, p. 12
Emmons Sea Worm, p. 13
Emmons Silvery Sides, p. 13

Emmons Slippery Squid, p. 13
Emu Bucktail Herring, p. 14
Emu Herring Grocery Fly, p. 14
Gee's Guitar Minnow (Bucktail), p. 15
Gee's Guitar Minnow (Clouser), p. 15
Holy Mackerel Clouser, p. 16
Jim's Grocery Mackerel, p. 16
Jim's Grocery Pollock, p. 17
Peacock Eel, p. 17
Rick's Murky Deceiver, p. 18
Sea Hag (Clouser), p. 19
Searun Muddler, p. 20
Sharp's Baby Herring, p. 20
Silverside Deceiver, p. 20
Wool-Head Deceiver, p. 22

Maine Sport Outfitters
U.S. Rt. 1, P.O Box 956
Rockport, ME 04856
Mail order: Flies, materials, tackle
Information and orders: (888) 236-8797;
fax (207) 236-7123
Online information/catalog:
www.midcoast.com/~mainespt
E-mail: mainespt@midcoast.com
Patterns: Holy Mackerel Deceiver, p. 16
Lunch, p. 1
Pola-Herring, p. 18
Walshie's Striper Fly, p. 21

Thom's of Maine
P.O. Box 932
Houlton, ME 04730
Mail order: Flies
Information and orders: (207) 532-4615
Patterns: Searsport Sand Eel, p. 19

• MARYLAND •

Chesapeake Fly & Bait Company
92 Jones Station Rd.
Arnold, MD 21012-1001
Mail order: Flies, materials, tackle; price list (free)
Information and orders: (410) 647-0445;
fax (410) 384-9410
Online information/catalog: www.chesapeakefly.com
E-mail: gr8flyz@chesapeakefly.com
Patterns: Chesapeake Gurgle Bug, p. 34
Chesapeake Sparkle Blue Crab, p. 35
Chesapeake Special, p. 35
Chesapeake Striper Special, p. 35
Hester's Brown & White Epoxy Sand Eel, p. 41
Hester's Brown Sea Worm, p. 41
Hester's Chartreuse Striper Streamer, p. 42
Hester's Floating Baitfish, p. 42
Punk Blonde, p. 45
Saltwater Grub, p. 46
Super Sea Ducer, p. 49

The Fisherman's Edge
1719 1/2 Edmondson Ave.
Baltimore, MD 21228
Mail order: Flies, materials, tackle; catalog (free)
Information and orders: (410)-719-7999 or
(800) 338-0053; fax (800) 338-0053
Online information/catalog: igofish.com or
chesapeakeangler.com
E-mail: flies@erols.com
Patterns: Bruce's Bay Anchovy, p. 30
Bruce's Crab Colored Deep Minnow (BCCCDM), p. 30
Bruce's Crab Colored Half & Half, p. 30
Bruce's Crystal Crab, p. 31
Bruce's Crystal Shrimp, p. 31
Bruce's Eel Fly, p. 32
Bruce's Epoxy Spoon Fly, p. 32
Bruce's Ultra Hair Silversides, p. 34

Lead Eyes Fly Company
13800 Fountain Rd.
Ocean City, MD 21842
Mail order: Flies, materials, tackle
Information and orders: (410) 250-3794
Online information/catalog:
www.oceancityfishing.com /charters/leadeye
(go to "charter boats/Lefco")
E-mail: lefco@ccisp.net
Patterns: Lefco Squid, p. 42

• MASSACHUSETTS •

The Bear's Den Fly Fishing Shoppe
98 Summer St.
Taunton, MA 02780
Mail order: Flies, materials, tackle
Information and orders: (508) 880-6226
Online information/catalog:
www.bearsdenflyfishing.baweb.com
E-mail: beardenfly@aol.com, or,
bearsden98@aol.com
Patterns: Bead Chain Fly, p. 9
Blue Bird, p. 10
Bow Tyer Arctic Fox Zonker, p. 10
Clondas—Crafty Critter, p. 11
Clondas—Kinky Angel, p. 11
Flat Wing Deceiver (Herring), p. 15
Scott's Shrimp, p. 19
Softex Squid, p. 21

First Light Anglers
17 Ashland Ave.
Manchester, MA 01944
Mail order: Flies, materials, tackle
Information and orders: (978) 526-4477;
fax (978) 526-8683
Online information/catalog:
www.first-light-anglers.com
Patterns: First Light Loligo, p. 74

• NEW HAMPSHIRE •

North Country Angler
Box 58
Intervale, NH 03845
Mail order: Flies, materials, tackle; catalog ($3)
Information and orders: (603) 356-6000;
fax (603) 356-9760
Online information/catalog:
www.northcountryangler.com
E-mail: angler@ncia.net
Patterns: Double Bunny Clouser, p. 11
Rhody Flat-wing, p. 18

• NEW JERSEY •

Coastal Guides Fly Shop
Forge Landing Marina Complex
Rte. 70
Brick Town, NJ
Mail order: Flies, materials, tackle
Information and orders: (732) 280-2249;
(732) 267-0058; (732) 929-9419
Online information/catalog: www.flyrod.net
E-mail: flyrodnj@aol.com
Patterns: Fly Rodders Widow, p. 39
Green Luster Grass Shrimp, p. 40
Mad Gails Mullet, p. 43
The Magician, p. 43
Pink Luster Grass Shrimp, p. 40
Sand Crab, p. 47
Spunks Bunks Silver Dollar, p. 48
Spunks Bunks Swimmer, p. 48

Delaware River Outfitters Ltd.
145 Rt. 13 N
Pennington, NJ 08534
Mail order: Flies, materials, tackle
Information and orders: (609) 466-7970;
fax (609) 466-7917
Online information/catalog: www.droltd.com
E-mail: deloutfitters@droltd.com
Patterns: C.S.'s Epoxy Spearing, p. 36
C.S.'s Hardhead Mullet, p. 37
C.S.'s Stealth Bunker, p. 37
C.S.'s Synthetic Peanut Bunker, p. 37
DRO Eel, p. 38
DRO Herring, p. 39

The Fly Fishing Shop
The Mall at Far Hills
P.O. Box 923
Far Hills, NJ 07931
Information: (908) 234-2232; fax (908) 234-9837
Patterns: Andy's 'Cuda Magnet, p. 25
Andy's Glow Squid, p. 25
Andy's Grass Shrimp, p. 25
Andy's Rain Fish, p. 26
Andy's Sand Eel, p. 26
Andy's Sand Flea, p. 26
Andy's Spearing, p. 27

The Fly Hatch
468 Broad St. Hwy. 35 So.
Shrewsbury, NJ 07702
Mail order: Materials, tackle
Information and orders: (732) 530-6784;
fax (732) 530-6838
Online information/catalog: www.flyhatch.com
E-mail: www.flyhatch.com
Patterns: Albie Slider, p. 23
Bozo Bunker, p. 29
Cute-Tip, p. 38
Sweet Cheeks, p. 50

North Country Outfitters
11 Rt. 15
Lafayette, NJ 07848
Mail order: Flies, materials, tackle
Information and orders: (973) 300-0344;
fax, (973) 300-1560
Online information/catalog:
www.northcountryoutfitters.com
Patterns: Bruce's Bunker, p. 30
Bruce's Herring, p. 33
Bruce's Sea-Ductive (Blue), p. 33
Bruce's Sea-Ductive (Chartreuse), p. 33
Bruce's Sea-Ductive (White), p. 33
Epoxy Bay Anchovy, p. 39

• NEW YORK •

The Camp-Site
1877 New York Ave.
Huntington Station, NY 11717
Mail order: Flies, materials, tackle
Information and orders: (516) 271-4969;
fax (516) 271-9621
Patterns: A.J.F. Back Bend (Herring), p. 23
Amedeo's Bluefish Squid, p. 24
Amedeo's Epoxy Squid, p. 24
Amedeo's Glow in the Dark, p. 24
Artistic Flies Spearing, p. 27
Bluefish Fly, p. 29
Don't Know Why, p. 38

The Tackle Shop, Inc.
Captain Harvey L. Bennett
P.O. Box 7033 Montauk Hwy.
Amagansett, NY 11930
Mail order: Flies, materials, tackle; catalog (free)
Information and orders: (516) 324-7770; fax (516) 324-3853
Online information/catalog:
E-mail:
Patterns: G&H Rock 'N'Roll, p. 40
G&H Touch 'N' Go, p. 40

Urban Angler, Ltd.
118 East 25th st., 3rd Floor
New York, NY 10010
Mail order: Flies, materials, tackle; catalog (free in U.S.)
Information: (212-979-7600
Orders: (800) 255-5488; fax (212) 473-4020
Online information/catalog: www.urban-angler.com
E-mail: urbang@panix.com
Patterns: Bushwick Special, p. 34

• PENNSYLVANIA •

Delaware River Anglers
228 Davisville Road
Willow Grove, PA 19090
Mail order: Flies, materials, tackle
Information and orders: (215) 830-9766
E-mail: schwam1@.com
Patterns: Slider Bug, p. 47
Yak Attack, p. 50

South Mountain Custom Rod & Tackle
Rd #4, Box 1365
Lebanon, PA 17042
Mail order: Flies, materials, tackle
Information and orders: (717) 964-3084
E-mail: jny@nbn.net
Patterns: Shenk's Pearly Killer, p. 47

• TEXAS •

Brazos Fly Fishers
4412 Waples Rd.
Granbury, TX 76049
Mail order: Flies, materials, tackle; catalog (free)
Information: (817) 279-1169; fax (817) 578-3626
Orders: (888) 200-0364
Online information/catalog: brazosflyfishers.com
E-mail: lhart@brazosflyfishers.com
rhart@brazosflyfishers.com
Patterns: Glass Bead Shrimp, p. 62
Hart Grass Shrimp, p. 66
Rattle Crab, p. 73
Rattle Mullet, p. 74

Cypert's Waterbugs, Inc.
Rt. 1, Box 128A
Aquilla, TX 76622
Mail order: Flies, materials; catalog on request (free)
Online information/catalog: www.waterbugs.com
E-mail: charlie@waterbugs.com
Patterns: Cypert's Minnow, p. 57
Cypert's Scissor Tail, p. 58
Cypert's Slim Jim, p. 58

Gruene Outfitters
1629 Hunter Rd.
New Braunfels, TX 78130
Mail order: Flies, materials, tackle
Information and orders: (830) 625-4440; fax (830) 625-4439
Online information/catalog: www.grueneoutfitters.com
Patterns: Chip's Fat Head Minnow, p. 54

Padre Outfitters
2400 Padre Blvd.
South Padre Island, TX 78597
Mail order: Flies, materials, tackle
Information and orders: (956) 761-2322; fax (956) 761-4241
Online information/catalog: www.padreoutfitters.com
Patterns: Chocolate Eel, p. 55
Flats Burger, p. 60
Lord Pinky, p. 69
Mr. Pinky, p. 71

• VIRGINIA •

Angler's Lab Outfitters
1554 Laskin Rd. #120
Virginia Beach, VA 23451
Mail order (phone or E-mail only): Flies, materials, tackle
Information: (757) 491-2988
Orders: (888) 732-8768; fax (757) 491-3413
E-mail: ronflyfish@aol.com
Patterns: Big Eye Clouser (Blue/White), p. 27
Big Eye Clouser (Sea Foam/Chartreuse), p. 28
Big Mac Clouser, p. 28
Black Death Clouser, p. 28
Clarabelle Clouser, p. 36
Clouser Minnow, p. 46
Mega Clouser (Blue/Green), p. 43
Mega Clouser (Chartreuse/White), p. 44
Mega Clouser (White), p. 44
Super Mullet, p. 48
Super Streamer (Anchovy Variation), p. 49
Super Streamer (Chartreuse/White), p. 49
Super Streamer (Sea Foam/Pink), p. 50

Severn Wharf Custom Rods
York River Yacht Haven
Gloucester Point, VA 23062
(mailing address:2702 Severn Wharf Rd. Hayes, VA 23072)
Mail order: Flies, materials, tackle
Information and orders: (804) 642-1972
Patterns: Mobjack Shrimp (Chartreuse), p. 44
Mobjack Shrimp (White), p. 45
Neil's Sparse Silverside, p. 45

Index of Originators and Tyers

Index of Fly Patterns

Pattern/Species Index

Boldface indicates that the pattern is tied primarily for the species.

Bonefish

Bonito

Boxfish

Cobia

Croaker

Dolphin

False Albacore

Flounder

Fluke

Jacks

Kingfish

Ladyfish

Speckled Sea Trout

Striped Bass